A Guide to

The Birds of the
Galápagos Islands

A Guide to
The Birds of the
Galápagos Islands

Isabel Castro and Antonia Phillips

Foreword by Peter R. Grant

Princeton University Press

Princeton, New Jersey

Published by Princeton University Press, 41 William Street,
Princeton, New Jersey 08540

In the United Kingdom, published by Christopher Helm (Publishers) Ltd.,
a subsidiary of A & C Black (Publishers) Ltd.,
35 Bedford Row, London WC1R 4JH

ISBN 0-691-01225-3

This book has been composed in Optima 10 pt

Printed and bound in Italy

3 5 7 9 10 8 6 4 2

CONTENTS

PREFACE

This book aims to gather together both the natural history of the birds of the Galápagos, and the characteristics that enable them to be identified in the field. Descriptions of all native, visiting and migratory birds reported for the archipelago and its surrounding waters are included.

It is written for everyone who visits the islands, whether on an organised tour or private trip, especially those with an interest in birds. It is hoped that the National Park guides will also find it useful. Finally, the book is also written for the people living in the Galápagos, to help them learn about and appreciate the unique and fascinating birdlife of the islands.

We should be grateful to hear of any omissions or comments on the contents of the book. In order to keep information up-to-date, we would appreciate news on further sightings. All correspondence should be addressed to Isabel Castro, Ecology Department, Massey University, Palmerston North, New Zealand.

FOREWORD by Professor Peter Grant

Most of us live on large land masses called continents, and when we visit remote islands we have a pleasant surprise. They are not just small versions of the continents we left behind, but are different in appearance and in the plants and animals they contain. This first became widely known from the accounts of travellers and early explorers, who brought back to Europe and later to North America tales of strange animals like dragons, and of the Dodo. Among the later travellers was Charles Darwin, and among the islands he visited was the Galápagos archipelago. Today, every traveller to the Galápagos is in a sense following in the footsteps of Darwin, experiencing the excitement of discovering the novelty and the strangeness of its wildlife.

Darwin's observations of the mockingbirds and finches were influential in his development of ideas about evolution, and specifically how new species were formed. But he was clearly puzzled by many features of them, and regretted he did not pay them more attention in his five week stay. We now have a much clearer idea than Darwin did of just why remote islands are biologically unusual, why a peculiar feature like flightlessness has evolved many times in many animals (birds and insects) in many islands around the globe, and why some groups of organisms are represented by several species and others by none.

Being remote, islands like the Galápagos are difficult to reach except by those creatures with good powers of dispersal, such as birds. Yet not all birds are born with equal powers of dispersal, and only a select few have been able to travel the long distance from the South American mainland in sufficient numbers to reach the islands and establish new populations. It is doubtful if parrots, toucans or hummingbirds, for example, have ever got to the Galápagos by their own wing power. And even if they did, how could they survive in an environment so different from the one they left behind? However, for the small number of bird species that crossed the Pacific and were able to found new populations the archipelago has been a paradise. That is why, with relatively few predators, competitors and parasites to contend with, they have generally become so common, and tame, why four mockingbird species evolved from one, and why as many as 13 finches have evolved from a single ancestral form in what appears to be less than three million years.

If islands around the world are to tell us much more than we already know there is some urgency in studying and conserving their native animals and plants because they are being lost at a higher rate than their continental relatives owing to human misuse of their environments. At least 100 species of birds restricted to islands have become extinct in the last four centuries, and we humans have probably had a hand in almost all these extinctions. The Dodo, for example, was observed by few westerners before it went extinct, and the moas were already gone from New Zealand well before the first people with white faces arrived. The Hawaiian archipelago has lost more than half of the 50 species of honey-creeper finches that evolved there. By comparison Galápagos has been fortunate. No species of bird is known to have become extinct, and nowhere else in the world is it possible to see an intact avifauna of comparable size. Yet even here populations are in a precarious state. The clearing of land for agricultural purposes, and the introduction of many alien plants, insects and mammals, has resulted in the disappearance of some bird populations on some islands. The rarest of Darwin's finches, the Mangrove Finch, is not secure in its islands of mangrove habitat around the coast of Isabela. Introduced rats, cats, anis and any new disease organism that might one day arrive in Galápagos can put the species, and not just a population of it, in jeopardy. This may already be happening.

Thus the birds of Galápagos are simultaneously fascinating in their uniqueness and a treasure to preserve. The archipelago possesses a cormorant that has given up the power of flight; a duck living on volcanic islands where fresh water is hard to find; a penguin and an albatross that would look more at home in the Antarctic; a finch that uses a spine or twig almost as long as itself to extract its food from beneath the bark of a tree, and another that sucks the blood of boobies; a species of petrel whose nest has never been found; and much more.

Isabel Castro has written a book that will help you to recognise them, learn about them and appreciate them for what they are and understand why we need to preserve them for the future. The book is the product of two years' of experience working with birds at the Charles Darwin Research Station on Santa Cruz island and visits to other islands. Helped by some fine illustrations it should serve as an excellent guide to the birds of Galápagos.

Peter R. Grant

ACKNOWLEDGEMENTS

We would like to thank Lindy Phillips for her unconditional support during the lengthy production of this book. In the early stages she provided us with a meeting place, wonderful food and company, and critical but encouraging words on our work.

Thank you to David Anderson, Glen Moll and Lindy too for making comments on the the first draft of this guide. This book was largely written in London, and grateful thanks are due to the librarians at the British Museum (Natural History) for their patience in locating essential papers and books used as references for the text. Mr David Rolstone kindly provided Isabel with a printer to obtain hard copies of the first drafts.

The Department of Ecology at Massey University allowed Isabel to work on the final drafts of this guide and to use the departmental facilities. Barbara Latch edited one of the final drafts of the text in record time and at a student price!

Thank you to the Natural History Museum, Tring and to the staff (and select residents!) of the Wildfowl and Wetlands Trust at Slimbridge for enabling Antonia to study and collect reference material for the illustrations. We are also grateful to Phil Batley for providing us with some wonderful slides of waders. Special thanks are due to Jeff Blincow for correcting the colour plates and for all his help and advice throughout the later stages of the project.

Finally we would like to thank Ellis Udy, and our families and friends for their encouragement during the production of this book—and the islands themselves for providing the inspiration and incentive.

Isabel Castro and Antonia Phillips
May 1996

INTRODUCTION

The word 'unique' is often overused, but not in the case of the Galápagos Islands. On arrival, your first sighting is likely to be a group of jet-black, dinosaur-like creatures, lounging on the rocky shore. Farther inland, the dry, red soil is broken by outcrops of lava. More bizarre reptiles, this time golden-grey in colour, feed upon fallen flowers beneath gigantic cacti. Look closer, and you see that some are apparently being groomed by small black or grey birds.

In the skies above, prehistoric-looking frigatebirds perform acrobatics, as they attempt to steal food from boobies, pelicans or gulls. It is hot and dry, and walking is exhausting, as the sharp lava rocks pierce your shoes.

Higher still, the view changes completely, with the rocky landscape being replaced by dense forest. Here are the massive tortoises, or 'Galápagos', that give the islands their name. Apart from the sound of mating tortoises, and the occasional call of birds, everything is still, for there are no indigenous mammals to break the silence.

Towards the top of the island the forest gives way to the pampas, an area of sedges, grasses and ferns, where rails add to the chorus of landbirds.

The archipelago, formed by 13 major islands and many islets and rocks, is located on the Equator, in the eastern Pacific, 1000 kilometres west of the South American coast. Like Hawaii, the islands have never been connected to any continent. Nine of the major islands are volcanoes or groups of volcanoes, some of which are still active, with volcano Fernandina last erupting as recently as February 1995.

Geologically speaking, the Galápagos Islands are very young: their age estimated to be between three and five million years. The total land area of the islands is about 8000 square kilometres.

The Galápagos archipelago was first discovered in 1535 by the Bishop of Panamá, Fray Tomás de Berlanga, who drifted off course while travelling to Peru. After the islands appeared on maps in 1570, they were used by buccaneers, whalers and pirates, for whom they provided refuge, water and food. During the 19th century, the first colonies were formed, and the islands were annexed by Ecuador, to which country they still belong.

Over the centuries, the archipelago has been known by many names: 'Insulae de los Galopegos', 'Encantadas', 'Archipiélago del Ecuador', 'Archipiélago de Colón', but the most common name has been 'Islas Galápagos.' The individual islands also have several names, though in this book we prefer the names most commonly used by the inhabitants.

The islands became famous after the visit of Charles Darwin in 1835. Much of Darwin's theory of evolution, a cornerstone of our understanding of the way the world works, was based on his observations of tortoises and finches on Galápagos. Since the publication of Darwin's *Origin of Species*, the islands have attracted the attention of scientists from all over the world. Today, they are said to be the world's greatest 'living laboratory'—not only for studying evolution, but also population dynamics, ecology and behaviour.

Although still a paradise, the islands have not been able to avoid the hazards

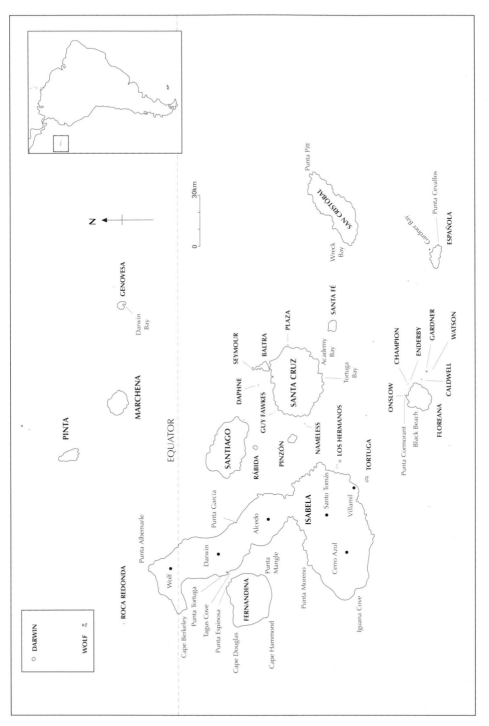

WOLF

DARWIN

ROCA REDONDA

Punta Albemarle

Cape Berkeley
Punta Tortuga
Tagus Cove
Punta Espinosa
Cape Douglas

FERNANDINA

Cape Hammond

Wolf

Darwin

Punta Mangle

Punta Moreno

Iguana Cove

Cerro Azul

ISABELA

Alcedo

Punta García

Santo Tomás

Villamil

LOS HERMANOS

TORTUGA

PINTA

MARCHENA

GENOVESA

Darwin
Bay

EQUATOR

SANTIAGO

RÁBIDA

PINZÓN

NAMELESS

DAPHNE

GUY FAWKES

SEYMOUR

BALTRA

PLAZA

SANTA CRUZ

Academy
Bay

Tortuga
Bay

SANTA FÉ

ONSLOW

CHAMPION

ENDERBY

GARDNER

WATSON

CALDWELL

FLOREANA

Punta Cormorant

Black Beach

SAN CRISTÓBAL

Punta Pitt

Wreck
Bay

Gardner Bay

Punta Cevallos

ESPAÑOLA

N

0 — 30km

12

of human colonisation. Introduced plants have altered the islands' native habitats, eliminating many native species. Introduced predators such as cats and rats have brought populations of reptiles and birds to the brink of extinction, and human activities continue to threaten the islands' ecosystems.

Evolution on Islands

Evolution is a process of gradual change over long periods of time, often best observed on islands, whose self-contained isolation makes them ideal for such a purpose.

The important aspects driving the evolutionary process on islands include their origin, degree of isolation, how long they have been isolated, their size and their age.

There are two kinds of islands: those that separated from a larger continental mass and those that were formed far from land as a result of volcanic activity or movements of the Earth's crust. The first kind, continental islands, generally remain close to the continent from which they separated, and so usually carry populations of the animals and plants from that continent.

The second kind, oceanic islands, have to be colonised by plants and animals. These islands may be very far from a continent, hence affecting the rate and kind of colonisation and the type of organisms that can arrive there. The Galápagos Islands are oceanic.

The water that surrounds an island acts as a barrier, making it difficult, and in some cases impossible, for organisms to arrive, and keeping them isolated from their counterparts on the mainland. To reach oceanic islands, animals and plants from the continent have to travel very large distances across the ocean. For some groups of organisms this is very difficult because the water is salty, and they become dehydrated before they can reach land. This is especially true for animals such as amphibians that require permanent skin moisture.

Mammals and reptiles have to first find a suitable way to cross the water, and second withstand the journey without fresh water and food. Insects, spores and seeds can be carried by winds, or ocean currents. Small birds and weak fliers may be transported to islands both by strong winds or rafts, but may also die in the process.

This aspect of isolation considerably reduces the number of possible founder species for oceanic islands. The farther the islands are from the source of colonists the smaller the number of species likely to arrive.

For those that make it to the island there is yet another ordeal: to establish themselves. No island is suitable for every organism that arrives there. For example, a plant may arrive but not its pollinator; or a plant's seed might reach the island alive, but may find no soil at all, or not the right soil in which to grow, or not enough water. Animals may not find the appropriate habitat for feeding or breeding; or simply not find the opposite sex. For animals with poor locomotion, if a female lands on one side of the island, and a male on the other, they may never meet.

The first vertebrates to reach oceanic islands are generally seabirds. These animals are used to long pelagic voyages, and islands are their favourite breeding grounds. Many seabird species do not require any special vegetation on which to place their nests—bare ground and rocks are enough.

Other early colonisers include bacteria, fungi, lichens and salt-tolerant plants. Their action upon the rocks, with the help of wind and water erosion, create the soil where higher plants can eventually grow. Once plants have established themselves on the island, landbirds, reptiles, and mammals can successfully colonise; even amphibians too (none present in the Galápagos archipelago), as long as they find fresh water and have plenty of luck!

Changes in the inherited characteristics that enable organisms to survive on the islands will eventually bring changes from the original, mainland population. For example, the New Zealand archipelago separated from the supercontinent Gondwanaland before mammals appeared. As a result, birds, insects and reptiles prospered, evolving new forms to occupy niches normally taken by mammals. For instance, wetas are large nocturnal insects that have evolved a lifestyle similar to that of mice.

On Galápagos, animals evolved without land predators and consequently are amazingly tame. Some birds, such as the cormorant, are flightless or spend a lot of their time on the ground. The Galápagos tortoises filled the niche that mammalian browsers have elsewhere. From the same reptilian ancestor, three species of iguana evolved: one able to feed on seaweed and dive beneath the icy sea, and another two land-based species capable of eating spiny cactus pads.

Life Arrives on the Galápagos Islands

Today there are 960 kilometres of ocean between mainland Ecuador and the nearest Galápagos island. When the first colonisers arrived, the islands must have been even farther from land. The tectonic plate on which the archipelago lies (Nazca Plate) is moving towards the South American continent, in an east-southeast direction, at a rate of about seven centimetres per year.

Although the islands, being so dry and covered by vast lava fields, are very hostile to visiting organisms, several features have aided colonisation. The northeast and southeast trade winds blow from the American continent towards the archipelago. Ocean currents also come from the continent along the Equator towards the islands. These two natural forces undoubtedly helped organisms to arrive. In addition, seabirds probably brought the seeds or propagules of most of the plants now living on the islands.

The altitude of the islands is also an important factor in the establishment and diversity of the wildlife. Eleven of the 13 main islands are volcanoes, whose peaks emerge from the ocean. Some of these volcanoes rise high above sea level, with volcano Wolf on Isabela reaching an altitude of more than 1700 metres.

Galápagos, being so far from the potential sources of inhabitants, and being so young in geological and evolutionary age, has less diversity compared to the similar sized areas of land on the continent.

Weather on the Galápagos Islands

The weather in Galápagos plays a very important role in the ecology, population dynamics and evolution of the islands' animals and plants. It is highly variable, changing from year to year and from island to island, and sometimes even within the same island. However, there is a pattern of two seasons, the hot season, starting in December and continuing into May, and the cooler garúa (misty) season, during the remaining months of the year.

The oceanography and climatology of the islands are highly complex, but are nevertheless worth describing in some detail, because they have such an important influence on the ecology of Galápagos birds. For a more complete understanding of the topic we would recommend referring to a number of references listed in the Bibliography.

Ocean Currents

Galápagos has been described as being located in 'one of the most extraordinary oceanic environments in the world', largely because so many ocean currents converge in this area. The direction of their circulation, set up mainly by the trade winds, is to the west. However, in the Galápagos region, this direction is modified by advections, local upwellings and surface heating.

The most important current is the Equatorial Undercurrent (EUC) or Cromwell Current, which surfaces to the west of the Galápagos, and is formed by cold, saline, food-rich waters. Together with local upwelling areas it provides rich foraging zones for organisms dependent on the ocean.

For example, the reproductive success of seabirds is directly linked to the quality and availability of food. However, the occurrence, strength and duration of this upwelling is unpredictable. As a consequence, most seabirds in Galápagos are opportunistic breeders, waiting for this upwelling to commence breeding. When the EUC surfaces, the west coasts of Isabela and Fernandina are suddenly rich in food, and the seabirds in the area take advantage of this to reproduce.

Other important currents that influence the archipelago's weather and its birdlife are the North Equatorial Current (Panama Current) which carries warm, low saline, tropical waters, and the South Equatorial Current (Humboldt or Peruvian Current) which carries colder, saline waters. The presence of both tropical and cold waters makes it possible for birds from both ecosystems to live in the same area. Galápagos is the only place in the world where penguins and tropicbirds can be found together!

How can these currents affect the climate? When the strong southeast trade winds in the Galápagos area blow over the cold waters of the Humboldt Current the air cools, pushing the warm air up. Where the cold air meets the warm air, an inversion zone is formed. The resulting condensation produces mist (in Spanish, garúa) in the lowlands and rain in the windward southeast-facing slopes of the highlands.

In turn, when the Humboldt Current and the southeast trade winds lose strength, and the Panama Current is predominant, the warmer waters heat up the air, breaking down the inversion layer. During this time occasional cloud formation brings heavy rain to both the lowlands and the highlands.

The Hot Season

This season, December to June, is hot (temperatures above 30°C), humid, and heavy rains may occur. During this period there are generally blue skies and the southeast trade winds are less strong. The ocean is calm and the temperature of the water can reach 27°C or more in the northeast. During this time of the year most of the plants flower and produce fruit, and the majority of insects reproduce.

In the presence of this abundance of food the landbirds can afford to breed. However, the annual rainfall is very variable, and prolonged droughts occur. When this happens, some species do not even attempt to breed. In certain years, known as 'El Niño years', the rainfall is unusually heavy, and lasts for a longer period than normal.

The Garúa Season

During this season, from June to December, the strongest current is the Humboldt. The southeast trade winds are very strong, the ocean is rough, skies are continuously overcast and both the air and the sea temperature decrease. On the southeastern slopes of the highlands there is almost constant rain, while the lowlands are covered by garúa.

However, the garúa evaporates very quickly and has little effect on humidifying the soil or allowing water to accumulate for drinking. During this time of the year landbirds with short breeding cycles reproduce in the highlands, while in the lowlands breeding stops. The upwelling of colder water, when this happens, brings plenty of fish and the seabirds benefit. This season is also unpredictable both in length and occurrence.

El Niño

This phenomenon, which usually occurs around the end of the year (September to December), has been explained in several ways, which are still under discussion. The most popular view suggests that it is the result of an oscillation of the ocean levels in the south Pacific Ocean caused by the strong trade winds. According to this theory, the trade winds push water west causing a lowering of the ocean level in the eastern South Pacific and a raising in the west. When the trade winds weaken, all the water flows back eastwards, causing a dramatic change in temperature. This produces changes in the weather, including heavy rainfall and warm temperatures both on land and at sea. The duration and strength of this phenomenon varies and cannot be predicted.

El Niño events disrupt life in the islands in many different ways, and play an important role in the evolution of the species there. The consequences vary for the different organisms, generally depending on the strength of the event. During El Niño events ocean productivity is reduced because the upwelled waters are mixed with warm water, becoming warmer and poorer in nutrients. The amount of light available for photosynthesis is reduced, as is the production of organic material used as food by the zooplankton. As the zooplankton decline, the fish living on them also suffer, and so on up the whole of the food chain. Although adult seabirds, at the top of the food chain, may die through starvation, chicks and juveniles are the worst affected. Since this phenomenon extends to the South American coasts from southern Colombia to northern Chile, the pelagic feeders also suffer from a lack of food.

Besides starvation, there are other aspects associated with El Niño events that can either cause nesting areas to be deserted, or lower the reproductive success of seabirds. Mosquitos have been blamed for mass desertions of nesting colonies by Blue-footed Boobies, Waved Albatrosses and possibly Great Frigatebirds. Also, rains have caused collapses and inundations of the nesting burrows of Dark-rumped Petrels, and the exaggerated plant growth associated with the rains may be responsible for the nesting failure of Waved Albatrosses.

Landbirds respond differently to the temperature change and rains. In a wet, hot climate insects prosper, and landbirds which feed on them benefit too. Many plants also thrive as do the animals that depend on them for food. In the case of mockingbirds and finches, El Niño events have been found to create suitable conditions for a longer breeding season.

An important aspect of El Niño is that it helps organisms from the South American continent to reach the islands—perhaps the way the ancestors of some of the endemic birds arrived. It also aids the native organisms to disperse to other islands within the archipelago.

The strongest El Niño event registered in the last century occurred in 1982–83, and had a great impact on both the seabirds and landbirds of Galápagos. The effects of this event on the different species of seabirds varied from low reproductive success to not even attempting to breed. Many birds also died of starvation. Surveys revealed the dramatic effects of this phenomenon: the population of penguins dropped by 80 per cent, and the cormorant population by 50 per cent.

The landbirds, however, responded in a very different way. The most successful finches reproduced up to seven times in the eight months that El Niño lasted. One pair laid 29 eggs and fledged 20 young. Birds were reproducing at the age of two-and-a-half to three months, almost two years earlier than normal! Mockingbirds also had a longer breeding season.

However, not all was positive: it is possible that the great mortality of adult mockingbirds on Genovesa Island in 1983, caused by mosquito transmitted avian-pox, was owing to the high density of mosquitos spawned by the favorable El Niño conditions. Also Curry and Grant pointed out that many nests were destroyed by the heavy rains. Birds such as the Galápagos Crake, that nest on the ground, may not have been able to nest at all.

Although mortality of some species of birds is high and reproductive success is reduced during El Niño events, most populations recover rapidly, though some, such as penguins, are slow to recover.

Altitudinal Gradients and Habitat Changes

The importance of the different vegetation types on the lifestyle and evolution of the islands' birds cannot be overemphasised. Plants provide food, shelter and nesting material and it is the abundance, lack or changes of these, which influence population dynamics and ultimately evolutionary processes. Unfortunately, when humans modify or destroy the plants of an area they may also destroy its animal species.

The composition of the plant community varies with altitude. The figure opposite shows the different vegetation zones on Santa Cruz Island as treated here. These vegetation zones may occur at different altitudes or not be present at all in other islands. It is important to note that there is a temperature gradient from the lowlands to the upper pampas zone. For every 100 metres ascent there is a 1°C drop in temperature, so while the coast may experience temperatures of 19°C during the garúa season, the pampa zone, at almost 700 hundred metres above sea level, would be experiencing only 12°C.

There are also marked differences in precipitation: while the lowlands receive very little rainfall for up to 12 months, the highlands are much wetter, with an average dry season of only four months. These differences in temperature and rainfall occur over very short gradients which results in many different habitats and therefore increases the possibilities for evolution to take place in a small area.

Vegetation Zones on Santa Cruz

The **coastal zone** (0–50 metres above sea level), arid zone or lowlands is characterised by plants that can tolerate both dry conditions and high salinity. Plants typical of this zone are mangroves (red *Rhizophora mangle*, black *Avicennia germinans*, button *Conocarpus erecta*, and white *Laguncularia racemosa*), cacti (*Opuntia, Jasminocereus* and *Brachycereus*), saltbush (*Cryptocarpus*), *Parkinsonia, Cordia, Croton, Sesuvium,* and *Scutia*. Most of these plants produce berries and seeds that are important food for the landbirds living in the area. An important feature of this zone is the presence of many tidal lagoons.

The **transitional zone** (50–200 metres above sea level) is a forest zone with trees such as guayabillo (*Psidium galapaguensis*), matazarno (*Pisidia cartagenensis*), and pega-pega (*Pisonia floribunda*) in the canopy, and bushes of *Bursera, Croton* and *Opuntia* in the understorey.

The ***Scalesia* zone** (200–450 metres above sea level) is a forest area where the only indigenous tree species is *Scalesia*, endemic to the islands. Currently the introduced guava (*Psidium guajaba*) and cinchona (*Cinchona succirubra*) trees are taking over the *Scalesia*. Because this zone is very humid, liverworts, lichens and mosses cover the branches of the trees. There is a cover of herbaceous plants on the ground and a few shrubs in the understorey. The zone has been greatly degraded by farming, which is a pity because this forest contains great diversity and supports many endemic bird species.

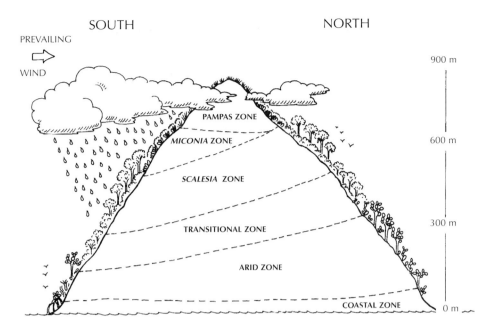

The ***Miconia* zone** (450–650 metres above sea level) is only present on the islands of San Cristóbal and Santa Cruz and is an area dominated by a shrub called *Miconia*. On both islands the zone is very reduced and in Santa Cruz the introduced *Cinchona* is invading this area, displacing the endemic *Miconia*.

The so-called **pampas zone** (650–850 metres above sea level), is a large area covered by ferns, grasses and sedges.

These last three zones receive considerably more water than the lowlands and transition zones and during the wet season many temporary pools are formed, housing a varied number of birds. Finally, it is important to mention that some islands comprise mainly bare lava unsuitable for vegetation.

It is important to point out that although the inhabited islands (past and present) have had their vegetation modified, several of the smaller islands and Fernandina are still pristine. However, there is always the threat of introduced seeds being transported by birds or in the shoes and clothes of locals, tourists or scientists. Our personal contribution to the conservation of the 'Enchanted Islands' could be to make sure we are not introducing seeds from one island to another.

Wetlands

Wetlands in the Galápagos are represented by fresh and saltwater ecosystems that can be either temporary or permanent. The **saltwater** bodies, except for intertidal pools, are mostly permanent. They are shallow lagoons, not exceeding one metre in depth, situated along the coast of all the islands. The main vegetation cover around the lagoons is mangrove. Other saltwater-resistant plants commonly found are saltbush (*Cryptocarpus pyriformis*), poison apple (*Hippomane mancinella*), *Parkinsonia*, *Opuntia* cactus, candelabra cactus (*Jasminocereus*), *Sesuvium*, palo santo (*Bursera graveolans*) and *Scutia*. The lagoons are fed by ocean water during high tides and rain water during the rainy season. Some may have underground connection with the ocean. Water evaporates during the dry season until desiccation sometimes occurs. Some of these lagoons are used as salt mines by the residents.

There are a large number of these lagoons, most of which are rarely visited, and little known. Some are of importance to tourism, including Punta Cormorant and la Montura on Floreana; Salinas and Cementerio on Isabela; Tortuga and Las Bachas on Santa Cruz; and Rábida on Rábida. Some are still not on the list of tourist sites and represent study areas for scientists and wildlife refuges. Examples of these lagoons are West Barahona, East Barahona, Tercera Playa, Cuarta Playa and Quinta Playa on Southern Isabela. This chain of lagoons is very important because it supports about 90 per cent of the islands' Greater Flamingo population. As well as offering breeding and feeding grounds for ten other resident bird species, they are one of the few untouched overwintering areas for many species of migrants.

Pintails and flamingos feeding in a lagoon on Floreana

There have been at least 50 different species of birds recorded on the saltwater lagoons, most of them migrants. Many others could be overlooked, either through lack of knowledge, or just because no observers are there at the right moment. Most reports of migratory birds have been by well known ornithologists visiting the islands. Because in many other parts of the world the wintering and breeding habitats of migratory species have been severely damaged, places such as the Galápagos are of great importance to their survival.

Although there has been little research on this topic, we know that the Galápagos is an important wintering area of Wandering Tattler (*Heteroscelus incanus*), a migrant that breeds in arctic regions. Some migrants such as Ruddy Turnstones and Sanderlings can be seen throughout the year. It is possible that immatures of these species stay on the islands until they reach maturity, then return to their place of origin to reproduce. Some migrants also use the freshwater lagoons of the highlands, where they feed on insects.

Freshwater wetlands are of three kinds: temporary pools, lagoons and a man-made reservoir. The vegetation around the freshwater lagoons is varied, and includes many introduced pest-plants such as blackberry (*Rubus*), guayaba (*Psidium guajaba*) and cinchona (*Cinchona succirubra*) trees. These bodies of water have low bird diversity when compared with the saltwater ones. Pintail ducks and gallinules are the only resident birds, while grebes may prove to be breeding there. Other migratory birds can be found only during certain times of year.

Temporary pools are formed during the wet season at sea level or during the garúa season in the highlands. These pools are important since they are essential for the successful breeding of the endemic Galápagos Crake and the Paint-billed Crake. They also provide feeding areas for waders and ducks.

El Junco and La Poza Colorada lagoons on San Cristóbal are the only two freshwater lagoons on the islands. La Poza Colorada, which is normally less than one metre deep, dried out during the prolonged drought of 1988–89, but will probably fill up again in the future. El Junco is 16 metres deep, and could be considered to be a small lake. The freshwater reservoir called La Toma, in the highlands of San Cristóbal, is also deep. Frigatebirds use La Toma and El Junco to bathe.

Conservation

The three main organisations involved in the conservation of the islands' flora and fauna are the Galápagos National Park Service, the Charles Darwin Foundation for the Galápagos Islands, through its research station, the Charles Darwin Research Station (CDRS), and the relatively new, UK-based, Galápagos Conservation Trust (GCT, P.O. Box 50, Shaftesbury, Dorset, SP7 8SB, UK). The Galápagos National Park Service (GNPS), which is part of the Ecuadorean Ministry of Agriculture and Livestock, is the institution in charge of the management of the National Park. This includes the creation and enforcement of rules and regulations, the development of protection and eradication projects, and the training of tour guides. The Charles Darwin Research Station advises the

GNPS on the management of the islands, by encouraging and developing conservation-related research. The CDRS also trains Ecuadorean students, offering voluntary positions and scholarships to carry out research on the islands, under the supervision of CDRS personnel. The GNPS and CDRS headquarters are located on Santa Cruz island.

Although the islands' wildlife is fully protected, there is still much to be done from a conservation point of view. The islands have no protection against introduced plants and animals that are still being brought ashore on cargo or private boats. More worrying is the lack of control of insects brought to the islands in the vegetable products used for human consumption. If disease-transmitting insects arrived, their effect on such a vulnerable environment as the Galápagos would be catastrophic.

Plants are introduced for both agricultural and ornamental purposes. These plants compete with the native flora, and are causing the disappearance of the original habitats where the islands' endemic animals evolved. Introduced plants can also have an adverse effect on wetlands, as on San Cristóbal, where introduced blackberry plants (*Rubus* sp.) are surrounding the El Junco lagoon. These plants are killing all the surrounding vegetation by overwhelming the local flora. If this thorny plant reaches the edges of the lagoon, it could wipe out the nesting habitat for Galápagos White-cheeked Pintail and Common Gallinule.

Drastic changes in habitats have caused the extinction of many bird species on other islands around the world, and prompt measures are necessary to prevent the same fate befalling the Galápagos. At present, particularly in the highlands of the inhabited islands, birds are facing problems because of the destruction of habitat for farming. Examples of threatened species include Galápagos Crake and Paint-billed Crake. In the agricultural zone of San Cristóbal crakes nesting in cattle pastures are under constant threat of being trampled by the animals' hooves.

Introduced mammals are another major problem. Not only do they interfere as predators, but they can also become competitors for food and habitat. Cats, dogs, pigs and rats feed upon eggs and nestlings, and even on adult birds and reptiles. Donkeys, goats, cattle and pigs trample the nests and eggs of ground-dwelling species, and compete with herbivores for food.

Although there are already two airports receiving jet flights seven days a week, a new airport has been built at Villamil, the port of Isabela island. This airport is located near the lagoons, and may harm birds both through noise and the increased number of tourists it will bring to the island. What effect this will have on the lagoons' continued survival is unknown. We do not know enough about this complex ecosystem so it is possible that losing even a single lagoon, however small, might cause irreversible harm to the birds.

The GNPS and CDRS have several programmes directed towards the eradication and control of introduced animals and plants. However, many of these are ineffective, owing to the lack of money and resources. The GNPS employs only around 60 park wardens, a very small number considering the task of protecting and managing such a huge area.

To conserve the Galápagos, so that evolution can continue without human interference, it is essential that laws to prevent further introductions are made.

All boats should be fumigated before they leave the continent, and inspected on arrival, to prevent the introduction of new plants and animals. The same procedure should be followed for boats travelling between the islands. Fishing boats should also be checked periodically for rats.

Galápagos National Park provides Ecuador with a large income from tourists, and has created jobs for many people. It is also a wonderful place to visit. However, if we wish to continue to enjoy this unique place we must make sure there is no further abuse: natural resources are renewable only until they are exhausted.

As well as the making and enforcement of laws, more effective educational programmes should be developed. Apart from their biologists, most Ecuadoreans are unaware of the global importance of the islands. Many of the immigrants from the continent are indifferent towards the fate of the islands' wildlife, and are only concerned with making a living. Soon the Park will have to face the inevitable consequences of a growing population: the need for more space to build houses, schools, a decent hospital and hotels. People must be aware that if they wish to continue living off the islands, they must keep them productive. The Galápagos will always have a human population living alongside the flora and fauna, but it is how the people choose to live, and how good they can make their relationship with the islands' wildlife, that will make all the difference to the survival of this unique ecosystem.

Fishing pelicans

Birding on the Galápagos Islands

Because the Galápagos archipelago is one of the few places in the world where the wildlife is not afraid of humans, birding there is a wonderful experience. Where else in the world would a bird stand on top of your binoculars while you are trying to observe it? Where else would you attract birds by being noisy instead of quiet? Where else would a bird take your hair, or shoelaces, as material for building their nests? Where else would an owl use you as a perch, or a hawk stand 30 centimetres away from you? All this, and more, has happened to us and to many other people with whom we have shared the privilege of living in the Galápagos. Even if your visit is too short to fully experience the tameness of all the islands' birds, you will still be overwhelmed by them.

Mockingbirds on the Galápagos are renowned for their curiosity

To observe most of the resident birds and many of the migrants it is necessary to stay on the islands for some time. A five to seven-day boat tour is the minimum time a birdwatcher should allow to observe a cross-section of the islands' species. However, to observe all the residents it is necessary to spend time in all the different habitats. For migrants, the season is also important. Most migrants are on the islands during the northern hemisphere late autumn and winter periods, from October to February, coinciding with the end of the dry season and beginning of the hot season. During this period all the landbirds reproduce (if there has been rain) and there is a lot of activity, making it an ideal time to plan your visit.

One of the major challenges on the islands is being able to see all the species of Darwin's finches. This is a very difficult task, as in many instances measurements are necessary to make sure which species you are looking at. However, spending long hours searching the right islands should eventually lead to a sighting of all the species. With perserverance, and a little luck, you may even manage to observe the use of a stick by a Woodpecker Finch, one of only a few tool using bird species. The following table gives information on where to find the different resident species.

Species	Islands	Habitat
Galápagos Penguin	Isabela, Fernandina, Bartolomé.	Coast
Waved Albatross	Española	Coast & ocean
Dark-rumped Petrel	San Cristóbal, Santa Cruz, Floreana, Santiago	Highlands** & ocean
Audubon's Shearwater	All islands*	Coast & ocean
Elliot's storm-petrel	At sea everywhere	Ocean
Wedge-rumped Storm-petrel	San Cristóbal, Genovesa, Isabela	Coast & ocean
Madeiran Storm-petrel	Isabela, Santa Cruz, Floreana, San Cristóbal, Plazas, Daphne, Genovesa & Bartolomé	Coast & ocean
Red-billed Tropicbird	Santa Cruz, Plazas, Santiago, North Seymour, Daphne & Genovesa	Coast & ocean
Magnificent Frigatebird	All islands	Coast
Great Frigatebird	Española, Fernandina, Isabela, Genovesa, San Cristóbal, Darwin, Wolf & North Seymour Sometimes at Rábida, Floreana & Santa Cruz	Coast
Blue-footed Booby	All islands	Coast
Masked Booby	All islands	Coast
Red-footed Booby	San Cristóbal, Genovesa, Wolf, Darwin, Marchena & Gardner Islet	Coast
Flightless Cormorant	Isabela & Fernandina	Coast
Brown Pelican	All islands	Coast
White-cheeked Pintail	All islands	Lagoons & temporary pools
Greater Flamingo	Floreana, Santa Cruz, Isabela, Santiago, Rábida & Bainbridge Rocks	Lagoons
Great Blue Heron	All islands except Marchena, Pinta, Wolf, Darwin	Coast, lagoons & towns
Great Egret	Isabela, Fernandina, San Cristóbal & Floreana	Higlands, coast, lagoons
Cattle Egret	Isabela, San Cristóbal, Santa Cruz & Floreana	Agricultural & coast
Striated Heron	Isabela, Santa Cruz, Fernandina, Pinzón & Pinta	Coast & lagoons
Lava Heron	All islands	Coast and lagoons
Yellow-crowned Night Heron	All islands except Wolf & Darwin	Coast, lagoons & towns
Galápagos Hawk	All islands except San Cristóbal, Genovesa, Wolf, Darwin & Marchena	Lowlands*** & highlands
Galápagos Crake	Santiago, Isabela, Santa Cruz, San Cristóbal, Pinta & Fernandina	Highlands
Paint-billed Crake	Santa Cruz, Isabela, Floreana, San Cristóbal & Genovesa (visitor)	Agricultural & lowlands
Common Gallinule	San Cristóbal, Santa Cruz, Isabela, Floreana & possibly Fernandina	Lagoons
American Oystercatcher	All islands	Coast
Black-necked Stilt	All islands	Coast & lagoons
Lava Gull	Santa Cruz, San Cristóbal, Isabela. Possibly on other Islands	Coast & lagoons
Swallow-tailed Gull	All islands except Fernandina	Coast
Sooty Tern	Darwin & Wolf; also at sea	Coast & ocean
Brown Noddy	All islands	Coast

Species	Islands	Habitat
Galápagos Dove	All islands	Lowlands
Dark-billed Cuckoo	Isabela, Fernandina, Santa Cruz, San Cristóbal, Floreana, Santiago & Pinzón	Lowlands & Transitional
Smooth-billed Ani	Isabela, Santa Cruz, Floreana & Santiago	Agricultural & lowlands
Barn Owl	Fernandina, Isabela, Santiago, Santa Cruz & San Cristóbal	Lowlands & highlands
Short-eared Owl	All islands except Wolf and maybe Rábida	Lowlands & highlands
Vermillion Flycatcher	All islands except Santa Fé, Rábida, Wolf, Darwin, Española, Genovesa & Baltra	Lowlands, agricultural & Scalesia
Galápagos Flycatcher	All islands except Genovesa, Darwin & Wolf	All zones
Galápagos Mockingbird	All islands except Española, San Cristóbal, Floreana & Pinzón	Lowlands & agricultural
Charles Mockingbird	Gardner & Champion Islets (Floreana)	Coast
Hood Mockingbird	Española and its satellite islet, Gardner	Lowlands
Chatham Mockingbird	San Cristóbal	Highlands & lowlands
Galápagos Martin	All islands except Wolf, Darwin, Marchena, Pinta, Rábida & Genovesa	Coastal & highlands
Large Ground-finch	All islands except Española and Daphne	Lowlands
Medium Ground-finch	All islands except Española, Genovesa, Wolf & Darwin	Lowlands & pampas, if dry
Small Ground-finch	All islands except Genovesa, Darwin, Wolf	Lowlands & highlands
Sharp-beaked Ground-finch	Fernandina, Santiago, Pinta, Genovesa, Darwin & Wolf	Miconia & Lowlands
Common Cactus-finch	All islands except Darwin, Wolf, Genovesa, Pinzón & Fernandina	Lowlands
Large Cactus-finch	Genovesa, Española & Gardner	Lowlands
Vegetarian Finch	All islands except Española, Genovesa, Santa Fé, Baltra, Darwin & Wolf	Coast to highlands
Large Tree-finch	All islands except Española, Genovesa, Wolf & Darwin	Highlands
Medium Tree-finch	Floreana	All zones
Small Tree-finch	All islands except Marchena, Española, Genovesa, Wolf & Darwin	Coast to highlands
Woodpecker Finch	Isabela, Fernandina, Santiago, Santa Cruz, Pinzón and San Cristóbal	Coast, Transitional & Scalesia
Mangrove Finch	Isabela	Mangrove swamps
Warbler Finch	All islands except Daphne	All zones
Yellow Warbler	All islands	All zones

* All islands = Isabela, Fernandina, Santiago, Bartolomé, Rábida, Santa Cruz, Pinzón, Baltra, North Seymour, Plazas, Santa Fé, Floreana, Española, San Cristóbal, Genovesa, Pinta, Marchena, Wolf & Darwin

** Highlands = Includes the Miconia, Scalesia and Pampas Zones

*** Lowlands = Includes Coast and Transitional Zones

Bird Topography

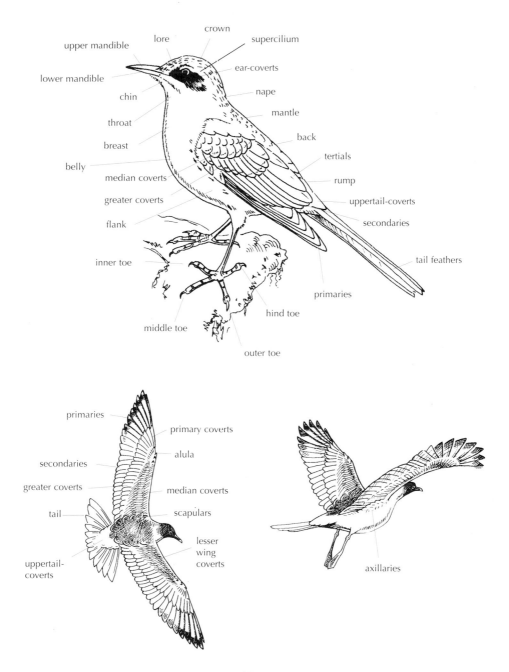

Evolution on the Galápagos Islands

Since Charles Darwin's visit in 1835, the Galápagos Islands have become world-famous for their place in his theory of evolution. This guide would not be complete without a brief reference to Darwin's work in the archipelago.

Darwin's finches have been used worldwide as 'classic' examples of the evolutionary process of speciation, through which new species form. Of the 14 finch species, 13 live on the Galápagos, and one on the Cocos Islands. They have all evolved from a single group of ancestors, though whether or not this ancestor first arrived on the Galápagos or Cocos Islands is not known. Nor do we know exactly where it came from.

However, the most interesting point about this bird is not where it came from, but that having arrived it separated into at least fourteen different species. This speciation can be explained as a result of three different processes: genetic drift (Lack, 1945), founder effect (Streseman 1936; Mayr 1963) and adaptive radiation (Lack 1945; Grant 1986).

David Lack's original adaptive radiation theory has been modified in the light of studies carried out by Peter and Rosemary Grant and their co-workers. According to them, a group of finch ancestors arrived on one of the islands about three million years ago. At that time, the Galápagos had many different habitats available, and the birds thrived there. Once the carrying capacity of the island had been reached, or possibly for other, unknown reasons, some of the birds moved to a neighbouring island or islands, where they became subject to slightly different selection pressures owing to the altered environment.

The main differences between the fourteen finch species are bill shape and size so the main selection pressures are represented by the different types of available food. Only those birds with bills that permitted them to eat the available food survived. The characteristics of the bill were genetically handed down from generation to generation, so after a period of time all the birds on the island looked the same. Then, some birds moved onto another island, where they were subject to slightly different selection pressures, favouring different characteristics. Over the centuries, this migration of birds from island to island continued. At times, immigrant birds would breed with residents, increasing the variation in the population. Sometimes, an immigrant group would arrive on an island where the residents were not feeding on part of the food supply, but which they were able to use. This was especially important during periods of food shortages. At these times, those birds that were able to specialise were more likely to survive, producing a selection pressure in favour of birds with a distinctive bill shape and size. The result was that individuals from each group tended to survive, finally dividing the two groups into two distinct species.

HABITATS

Wet Coastal Areas   Plate p. 30

In the wet coastal areas, mangrove thickets outline many of the islands. Saltwater lagoons provide shelter for an abundance of shorebirds, and the shallow waters contain a rich supply of food for the four species of heron, egrets, ducks, flamingos, and the Brown Pelicans which lurk above. Numerous migrant plovers, sandpipers and other waders also frequent these wetland areas.

Dry Coastal Areas   Plate p. 31

A diverse assembly of seabirds greets visitors on the bare lava cliffs and rocky beach areas. Most resident and endemic species can be seen in a week's visit, including three species of booby, two frigatebirds, gulls, terns, tropicbirds and Waved Albatross. On the rocky shores, Flightless Cormorants and Galápagos Penguins make their nests. Offshore, pelicans and boobies dive for fish, while American Oystercatchers and Galápagos Doves search the beach area for food.

The *Scalesia* Zone   Plate p. 32

In this lush cloud-forest habitat, dominated by *Scalesia* trees, the stillness is often broken by birdsong. Galápagos landbirds are a pleasure to watch, and their boldness and curiosity unequalled. Here, in the highlands, are mockingbirds, two species of flycatcher, Yellow Warblers, Dark-billed Cuckoos, Smooth-billed Anis and the shy Paint-billed Crake. Many species of finch, including Vegetarian Finch and the tool-using Woodpecker Finch, also frequent the misty highlands.

The *Miconia* Zone   Plate p. 33

The endemic *Miconia* forms a dense, shrubby area at this high level. These moist conditions favour sedges and ferns, under which the secretive Galápagos Crakes scurry around. The fearless Galápagos Hawk, two species of owl, several finch species and Galápagos Martin may be seen here. In the lower areas, temporary pools formed during the garúa season hold feeding White-cheeked Pintails, gallinules and waders.

Paint-billed Crake

Sora Rail

imm.

Pied-billed Grebe

Galápagos Crake

Purple Gallinule

Common Gallinule

Red-billed Tropicbird

ad. breeding

ad. breeding

Brown Pelican

non-breeding

Flightless Cormorant

♀

♂

♀

♂

Galápagos Penguin

ad.

imm.

Audubon's Shearwater

Dark-rumped Petrel

chick

Dark-rumped Petrel chick

Waved Albatross

Waved Albatross

36

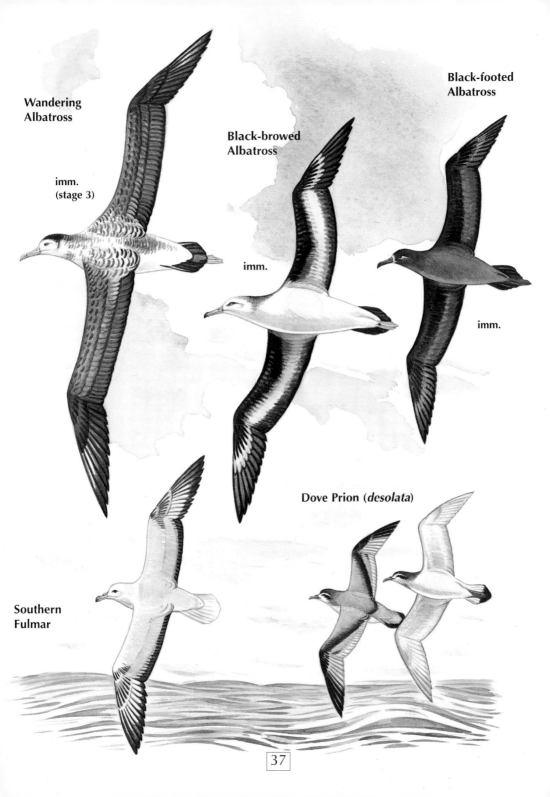

Wandering
Albatross

imm.
(stage 3)

Black-browed
Albatross

Black-footed
Albatross

imm.

imm.

Dove Prion (*desolata*)

Southern
Fulmar

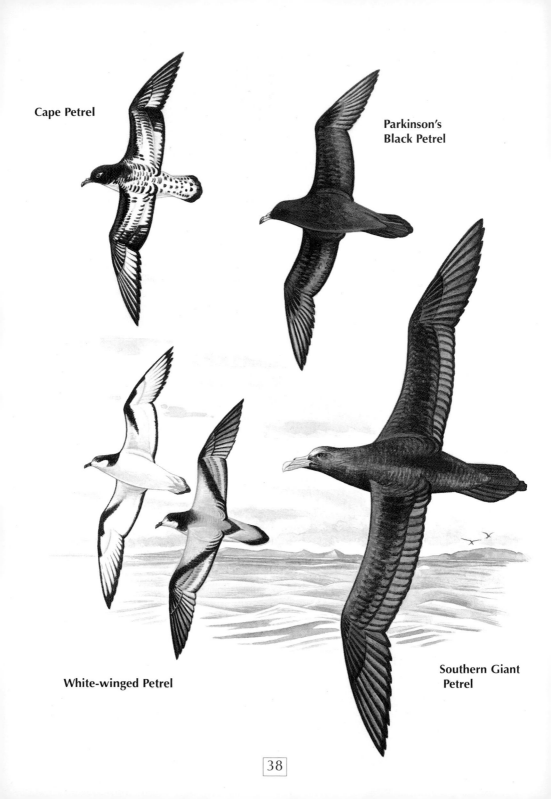

Cape Petrel

Parkinson's
Black Petrel

White-winged Petrel

Southern Giant
Petrel

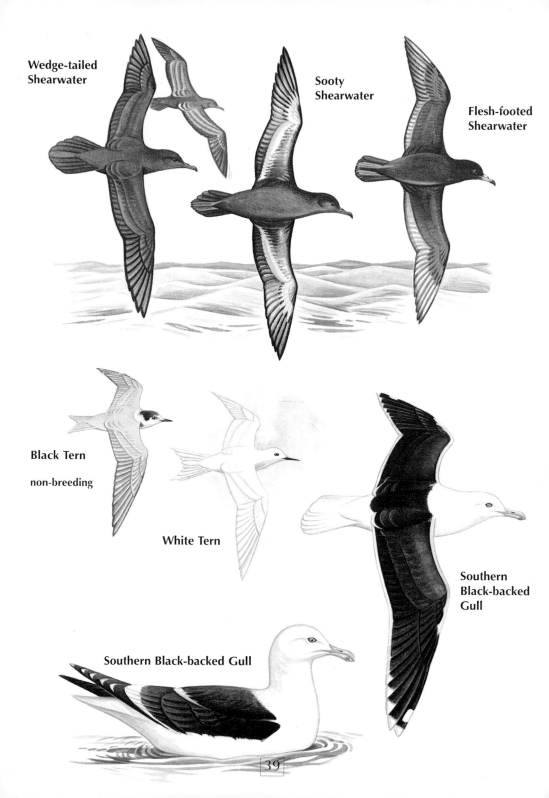

Wedge-tailed
Shearwater

Sooty
Shearwater

Flesh-footed
Shearwater

Black Tern

non-breeding

White Tern

Southern
Black-backed
Gull

Southern Black-backed Gull

Elliot's Storm-petrel

Madeiran Storm-petrel

Wedge-rumped Storm-petrel

40

White-faced
Storm-petrel

White-bellied
Storm-petrel

Leach's
Storm-petrel

Black
Storm-petrel

Markham's
Storm-petrel

Masked Booby

Blue-footed Booby display

Masked

Blue-footed Booby

Red-footed Booby

brown phase

white phase

Blue-footed

Red-footed

Great Frigatebird

Magnificent Frigatebird

Great Frigatebird

♂

♀

♀

♂

Great Frigatebird

♀

♂

♀

Magnificent Frigatebird

Great Frigatebird

imm.

imm.

Magnificent Frigatebird

Magnificent Frigatebird

Blue-winged
Teal

♂

Blue-winged
Teal

♂

White-cheeked
Pintail

White-cheeked
Pintail

Greater
Flamingo

Black-bellied
Whistling-duck

43

Great Egret

Cattle Egret

imm.

breeding

Great

Snowy Egret

Snowy

Cattle

non-breeding

44

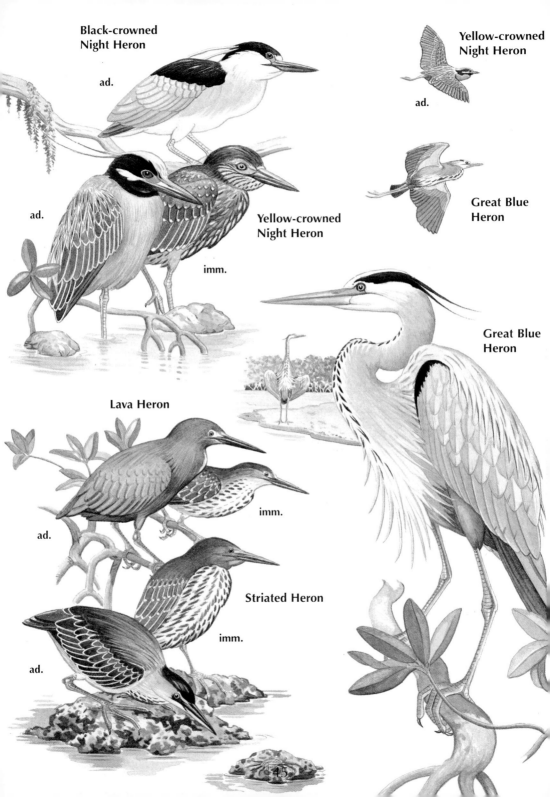

Black-crowned Night Heron

ad.

Yellow-crowned Night Heron

ad.

ad.

Yellow-crowned Night Heron

imm.

Great Blue Heron

Great Blue Heron

Lava Heron

imm.

ad.

Striated Heron

imm.

ad.

Galápagos Hawk

ad.

ad.

imm.

Osprey

ad. ♂

Peregrine
Falcon

Barn
Owl

Short-eared Owl

Solitary Sandpiper

non-breeding

breeding

Marbled Godwit

breeding

non-breeding

Sanderling

non-breeding

breeding

Least Sandpiper

breeding

non-breeding

Red Knot

non-breeding

non-breeding

Pectoral Sandpiper

breeding

breeding

47

Lesser Yellowlegs

Lesser
Yellowlegs

Greater
Yellowlegs

Whimbrel

Greater Yellowlegs

Whimbrel

Black-necked
Stilt

American Oystercatcher

48

Surfbird

breeding

non-breeding

Wandering Tattler

non-breeding

breeding

Short-billed Dowitcher

non-breeding

breeding

non-breeding

breeding

Spotted Sandpiper

non-breeding

breeding

Stilt Sandpiper

non-breeding

breeding

Willet

49

White-rumped Sandpiper

non-breeding

breeding

Baird's Sandpiper

non-breeding

breeding

Semipalmated Sandpiper

non-breeding

breeding

Western Sandpiper

non-breeding

breeding

Black Turnstone

non-breeding

breeding

Ruddy Turnstone

non-breeding

breeding

Red-necked Phalarope

non-breeding

Wilson's Phalarope

non-breeding

Red Phalarope

non-breeding

Semipalmated Plover

non-breeding

breeding

Wilson's Plover

breeding

non-breeding

Killdeer

non-breeding

breeding

American Golden Plover

non-breeding

breeding

breeding

non-breeding

Black-bellied Plover

Pomarine Skua

South Polar Skua

Franklin's
Gull

1st-winter

Franklin's
Gull

1st-winter

Laughing
Gull

1st-winter

Laughing
Gull

1st-winter

imm.

defensive posture

Lava
Gull

ad.

Lava
Gull

ad.

ad. non-breeding

ad. breeding

Swallow-tailed Gull

ad. breeding

Swallow-tailed
Gull

imm.

Royal Tern

non-breeding

Common Tern

Sooty Tern

Common Noddy

ad.

ad.

imm.

ad.

54

Galápagos Dove

Smooth-billed Ani

♂

Black-billed Cuckoo

Dark-billed Cuckoo

Belted Kingfisher

♀

♂

Common Nighthawk

Vermillion Flycatcher

♂

♀

Galápagos Flycatcher

♂

Eastern Kingbird

Yellow Warbler

♀

♂

Blackpoll Warbler

1st-winter

56

Bobolink

breeding ♂

non-breeding ♂

Indigo Bunting

Rose-breasted Grosbeak

♀

1st-winter

♂

♂

Summer Tanager

Cedar Waxwing

Red-eyed
Vireo

Galápagos Mockingbird

Chatham Mockingbird

Charles Mockingbird

Hood Mockingbird

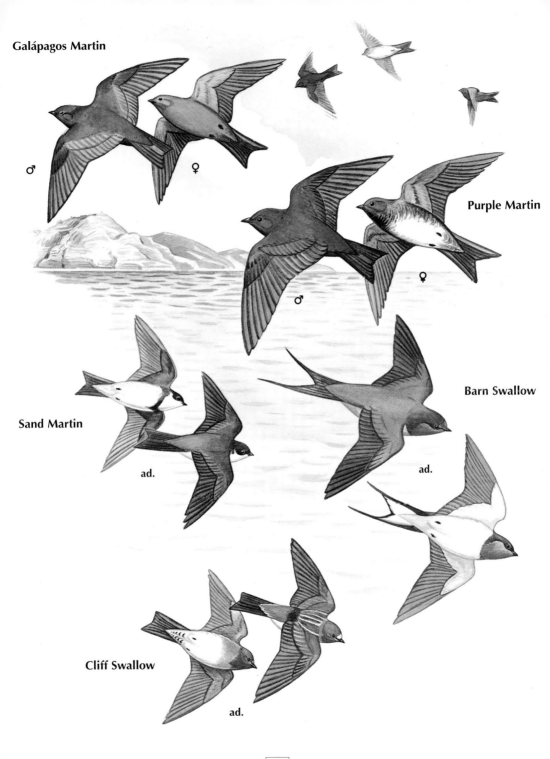

Galápagos Martin

♂

♀

Purple Martin

♂

♀

Sand Martin

ad.

Barn Swallow

ad.

Cliff Swallow

ad.

Large Ground-finch

ad. non-breeding

♂ ad. breeding

Medium
Ground-finch

ad. non-breeding

♂

♀

♂ ad. non-breeding

Medium
Ground-finch

Small
Ground-finch

ad. non-breeding

Sharp-beaked
Ground-finch

♂

♂

Common
Cactus-finch

♀

♂

Large
Cactus-finch

Large
Tree-finch ♂

Medium
Tree-finch ♂

Small
Tree-finch ♂

♀

Woodpecker
Finch

Mangrove
Finch

Vegetarian
Finch

Warbler
Finch

ORDER PODICIPEDIFORMES

Family Podicepedidae

Grebes are diving birds with flat lobes around their toes, legs far back on their bodies and short tails and wings. When flying, the head is held low. Only one species, Pied-billed Grebe, is found on the Galápagos.

PIED-BILLED GREBE *Podilymbus podiceps*   Plate p. 34

Sp: Somormujo

STATUS: Migrant.

IDENTIFICATION: Length 34 cm, wingspan 60 cm. Small, plump-looking grebe, with a short neck, large head, 'tailless' appearance, and thick, heavy bill. Plumage mainly greyish-brown, with white chin and white undertail-coverts. In breeding plumage has black band across bill. Dives frequently, and can be very secretive and difficult to see.

DISTRIBUTION: This grebe is a common species in South America, and has been recorded on a few of the brackish water lagoons of Isabela, Floreana and Santa Cruz, and on the freshwater lagoons of San Cristóbal. With its habits and breeding requirements, this species is a good candidate to colonise the Galápagos—indeed, given the reports of birds staying all year round, and sightings of immatures, breeding may already have occurred.

ORDER SPHENISCIFORMES

Family Spheniscidae

Penguins are chubby and flightless, with dark upperparts and white underparts. The only representative of the group within the islands is Galápagos Penguin, which is considered a vulnerable species.

GALÁPAGOS PENGUIN *Spheniscus mendiculus*   Plate p. 35

Sp: Pingüino de Galápagos

STATUS: Endemic.

IDENTIFICATION: Length 53 cm. This is the only penguin to live and breed as far north as the Equator. The adult has black wings and upperparts, and white underparts, with a black line running from the upper breast, down the flanks to the tail. The face is black, with a white line running through the eye, down the cheeks and across the base of the throat. The male is heavier than the female. The immature is grey where the adult is black, and lacks the head and chest markings. Chicks are completely grey. Usually found in small groups (two to seven birds), although when the water temperature is lower than 23°C, the groups in the water can comprise up to 20 birds.

DISTRIBUTION: Only found along the coasts of Fernandina, the west and northeast coasts of Isabela, Bartolomé's Pinnacle Rock, Sombrero Chino, Rábida, and sometimes along the coasts of Floreana and northern Santa Cruz (Guy Fawkes

Islands). According to the most recent censuses, the population is estimated at around 1400 to 2700 birds.

BREEDING: Galápagos Penguin breeds only on Isabela and Fernandina. The species is an opportunistic breeder, with a six-month breeding period. Pairs can produce up to three clutches a year. Reproduction depends on food availability, which in turn depends on water temperatures being below 23°C. The penguin moults feathers before breeding in a process that takes two weeks. It nests in burrows, crevices among the rocks, holes etc. Two eggs are usually laid, which are incubated by both parents for a period of about 40 days. Normally, only one of the chicks fledges, and the parents will take care of the chick for just under 60 days, until it is ready to go it alone. The pair bond is less permanent than in other penguin species.

FOOD: Feeds on fish and crustaceans.

ORDER PROCELLARIIFORMES

These are the true seabirds, or 'tubenoses', so called because of their external tube-shaped nostrils which enable them to survive on salt water during their long periods spent living out at sea. They are generally very faithful to their nesting site and mate, and are colonial nesters. They apparently use a heightened sense of smell to find their way to sources of food and to get back to their breeding grounds, which are generally near their birthplace.

Dark-rumped Petrel is in severe danger, being the only Galápagos bird that merits 'endangered' status in the *Red Data Book*. It has come to the brink of extinction owing to predation by introduced mammals, especially rats, cats, dogs and pigs. The GNPS and the CDRS, with funding provided by the World Wide Fund for Nature, are making enormous efforts to increase and maintain a high fledging success at the largest colony of this species on Floreana.

Another group, supported by the Audubon Society as well as the GNPS and CDRS, is trying to attract birds on Santa Cruz to safer nesting areas, by using playbacks of recorded vocalisations. There are plans to expand the project to other islands where the birds are known to nest, though this is dependent on further funding.

Wedge-rumped Storm-petrel, endemic at subspecies level, is known to nest at only three locations in the archipelago. One, a small islet about a quarter of a mile from land, has been invaded by black rats, causing heavy mortality of nesting birds for the past few seasons. Although this species is abundant at other nesting sites, the drastic drop in numbers in such a short time shows that it is necessary to monitor the different populations closely.

Feral cats and dogs are known to predate on seabirds on the larger islands. Their effect on the different species depends both on the numbers of predators and prey, and also on the climatic conditions which affect their feeding habits. It is known that during dry years cat predation on Dark-rumped Petrels increases, affecting the fledging success by about 30 per cent.

Family Diomedeidae

WANDERING ALBATROSS *Diomedea exulans*   **Plate p. 37**
Sp: Albatros Paseador
STATUS: Vagrant.
IDENTIFICATION: Length 107–135cm, wingspan 254–351 cm. A majestic seabird, breeding on subantarctic islands and in New Zealand; circumpolar in distribution. Acquires adult plumage through a number of stages, and is often difficult to separate from Royal Albatross in all plumages. In general, adults of both species have white body and head, white upperwings and blackish-brown primaries. Immatures have varying amounts of brown on body, head and upperwings. In immature Wandering, upperwings whiten from the centre outwards to leading edge of wing, in Royal from the leading edge inwards. Tail sides in Wandering are generally black, white in Royal. Wandering often follow fishing boats, a habit not shared by Royal. Recorded twice, though specific identification not established.

WAVED ALBATROSS *Diomedea irrorata*   **Plate p. 36**
Sp: Albatros de Galápagos
STATUS: Endemic.
IDENTIFICATION: Length 90 cm, wingspan 235 cm. The largest bird in the Galápagos, and unmistakable. A huge, long-winged seabird, with pale head, neck and upper breast, shading to buffish-yellow on the crown and back of neck. Underparts barred with dark brown. Upperwings and back dark brown; underwings white, fringed with brown. Bill huge and yellow; legs and feet grey. Male larger than female. Immature very like adult, but duller. Downy chicks can be brown, almost white, or any shade in between.
DISTRIBUTION: Endemic to Española, where it breeds from March to January every year. Breeding has also been reported from Isla de la Plata, off the mainland of Ecuador. From January to March, the breeding birds join the non-

breeders in the waters off the coasts of Ecuador and Peru.

BREEDING: Mates for life, and breeds annually. Birds perform an intricate courtship dance that takes place at the end of the breeding season. This dance is longer and more complex in new couples, or with an established pair which has failed to reproduce. By the end of March, birds have returned to Española for the breeding season. First to arrive are the males, who return to a place near the territory of the previous year. Any other bird that approaches the area is attacked. When the female arrives, mating takes place without any aggression.

Part of the elaborate courtship dance of Waved Albatross

Waved Albatross does not make a nest, the female simply laying a single white egg on the bare ground, which it incubates for 60 days. The parents share in the incubation, and both feed the chick until it fledges some 170 days after hatching. The fledglings reach maturity and return to breed when they are six years old.

FOOD: Feeds mainly on squid, fish and crustaceans.

BLACK-FOOTED ALBATROSS *Diomedea nigripes*   Plate p. 37

Sp: Albatros de Piés Negros

STATUS: Vagrant.

IDENTIFICATION: Length 68–74 cm, wingspan 193–213 cm. Adults mostly dark brown, except for white at base of bill and tail, and white vent (lower belly) and undertail-coverts. Immatures are wholly sooty-brown, except for faint white at base of bill. Recorded once in the waters between Galápagos and the mainland.

BLACK-BROWED ALBATROSS *Diomedea melanophris*

Plate p. 37

Sp: Albatros de Ceja Negra
STATUS: Vagrant.
IDENTIFICATION: Length 83–93 cm, wingspan 240 cm. Adults mostly sooty-brown on upperwings, primaries and leading edge of underwings. Body and head white, bill yellowish-orange, and a 'smudged' dark eyebrow. Immatures generally have more brown on underwing and across neck, and greyish bills. Recorded once in the archipelago's waters.

Family Procellariidae

This group includes the fulmars, shearwaters and larger petrels.

SOUTHERN GIANT PETREL *Macronetes giganteus*   **Plate p. 38**

Sp: Petrel Gigante Común
STATUS: Vagrant.
IDENTIFICATION: Length 86–99 cm, wingspan 185–205 cm. Adult greyish-brown, with whitish breast and head. Underwings slightly lighter in colour, with silver-grey secondaries. Immatures range from blackish-brown to light brown, less white on head and underwings than adult. A single record from the archipelago.

SOUTHERN FULMAR *Fulmarus glacialodes*   **Plate p. 37**

Sp: Petrel Plateado
STATUS: Vagrant.
IDENTIFICATION: Length 46–50 cm, wingspan 114–120 cm. A grey-and-white bird, with whitish head, grey upperparts and whitish underparts. Upperwings bluish-grey, with blackish primaries. Underwings mostly white, except for dark alula and slightly darker trailing edge. Tail grey above, white below. Recorded once in the Galápagos.

CAPE PETREL *Daption capense*   **Plate p. 38**

Sp: Petrel del Cabo
STATUS: Vagrant.
IDENTIFICATION: Length 39 cm. Highly distinctive, medium-sized petrel, with blotchy brown-and-white upperwings, white underparts and a dark head. Observed halfway between Genovesa and Marchena in 1961. Commonly seen in the waters between the Galápagos and the coast of Ecuador.

WHITE-WINGED (GOULD'S) PETREL *Pterodroma leucoptera*
Plate p. 38

Sp: Petrel de Gould
STATUS: Vagrant.
IDENTIFICATION: Length 30 cm. Medium-sized, long-winged 'gadfly' petrel. Upperwings show a distinctive brown and grey pattern, with dark head and tip of tail. Underparts mainly white, apart from dark fringes to wings and carpal bars. Has been seen in the ocean off the archipelago.

DARK-RUMPED (HAWAIIAN) PETREL *Pterodroma phaeopygia phaeopigya*
Plate p. 36

Sp: Patapegada
STATUS: Resident (endemic subspecies).
IDENTIFICATION: Length 43 cm, wingspan 91 cm. Large, long-winged petrel, with dark brownish-black upperparts, white underparts and a distinctive white forehead. Dark patch on neck extends down sides of breast. Bill thick and black. Underwings mainly white, fringed with dark brown along edges.
DISTRIBUTION: During the breeding season, may be seen at the colonies in the highlands of San Cristóbal, Santa Cruz, Santiago and Floreana (NB: this needs special permission from the SPNG). It may also be seen at dawn and dusk, flying near the shoreline of these islands, and also Pinta and Isabela. Finally, you may be lucky and observe one flying by at sea.
BREEDING: There are at least three different populations in the Galápagos, which reproduce at different times of the year, and have slightly different adult morphology. The population breeding on Santiago is of intermediate size, and breeds from January to October. The population on Floreana is larger in size, and breeds from October to August. Finally, the birds on Santa Cruz are smallest, and breed from March to January. The species mates for life, and the pair returns to the same nest year after year, nesting in burrows. The male usually arrives first at the colony, followed by the female. At the beginning of the season the burrows are visited by one or both birds, to remove the debris collected since they were last used, and in some cases to enlarge or elongate the chamber. Birds breeding for the first time start by searching for a mate, and a suitable place for a burrow. Copulation takes place at night, in front of the burrow. A single egg is laid, and incubated for around 50 days, with both parents involved. Both parents also feed the youngster until it is ready to fledge, some five months after hatching. Once fledged, the petrel takes five or six years to reach maturity.
FOOD: Adults feed mainly on squid, fish and crustaceans. The nestling is fed regurgitaed food, made up of partially digested fish, crustaceans and squid combined with oil.

DOVE PRION *Pachyptila desolata* **Plate p. 37**
Sp: Petrel Ballena
Status: Vagrant.
Identification: Length 25–30 cm, wingspan 57–66 cm. Head bluish-grey, with white superciliary emphasised by blackish stripe under eye, stretching to ear-coverts. Upperparts blue-grey, with blackish bar across lower back; underparts white. Upperwings bluish-grey, with distinct black 'M' running from wingtip across wing to lower back. Underwings are mostly white. Tail is bluish-grey with black tip. Only record is of a single dead bird found on Floreana.

PARKINSON'S BLACK PETREL *Procellaria parkinsoni* **Plate p. 38**
Sp: Petrel de Parkinson
Status: Vagrant.
Identification: Length 46 cm. Large, wholly dark petrel, with blackish-brown plumage apart from pale primary shafts on the underwing. The only records date from an expedition in 1905.

WEDGE-TAILED SHEARWATER *Puffinus pacificus* **Plate p. 39**
Sp: Pardela del Pacífico
Status: Vagrant.
Identification: Length 43 cm. Large, long-winged, wholly dark shearwater with a distinctive wedge-shaped tail, broad wings and a buoyant flight. Has been observed to the northwest of the islands. One specimen also found on Plazas in a Short-eared Owl pellet. Common in the ocean between the Galápagos and Panama.

FLESH-FOOTED SHEARWATER *Puffinus carneipes* **Plate p. 39**
Sp: Pardela Negruzca
Status: Vagrant.
Identification: Length 43 cm. Large shearwater, wholly blackish-brown apart from silvery bases of primaries on underwing (only evident in good light). Distinguished from Wedge-tailed by straighter wings, generally held forward. Reported from Isabela and Pinzón during October to January.

SOOTY SHEARWATER *Puffinus griseus* **Plate p. 39**
Sp: Pufino Negro
Status: Vagrant.
Identification: Length 44 cm. Large shearwater with long, narrow wings and wholly dark plumage. Silvery-white wing-linings are distinctive. Flight fast, with stiff wings. Reported from South Isabela, Genovesa and Pinzón, in most cases associated with El Niño events (see Introduction).

AUDUBON'S SHEARWATER *Puffinus lherminieri subalaris*

Plate p. 36

Sp: Pufino

STATUS: Resident (endemic subspecies).

IDENTIFICATION: Length 30 cm, wingspan 69 cm. Small shearwater, with brownish-black upperparts and crown, and white underparts. Underwings show white central strip, surrounded by brown. Often rests on the surface of the sea. May be confused with Dark-rumped Petrel, but shearwater is smaller, with dark forehead, shorter wings and thinner bill.

DISTRIBUTION: Usually seen near cliff faces, feeding together with Brown Noddies and storm-petrels, off all the islands.

BREEDING: Breeds in small colonies throughout the year, in cycles of seven to 11 months. Moulting usually takes four to five months, but birds will abandon their moult sequence and attempt breeding if conditions become favourable. The shearwater usually nests among rock cavities in the cliff face where it lays a single egg, which compared to the female's weight is very large. The egg is incubated for an average of 51 days by both parents, who also feed the young, for an average of 75 days, until the bird fledges.

FOOD: Feeds by plunge-diving, to a depth of at least two metres, The main food items are planktonic larval fish, crustaceans, squid and tiny fish.

Family Hydrobatidae

Storm-petrels are small, generally dark birds that flutter over the surface of the waves in search of food. All three species found in the Galápagos are similar in size and appearance, being dark with white bands around the rump, making them difficult to tell apart. To identify them successfully, special attention must be paid to the size and shape of the rump band, the location, time of day and their feeding behaviour.

ELLIOT'S STORM-PETREL *Oceanites gracilis galapagoensis*
Plate p. 40

Sp: Golondrina de Tormenta de Elliot

STATUS: Resident (endemic subspecies).

IDENTIFICATION: Length 15 cm, wingspan 40 cm. The smallest storm-petrel of the islands. Superficially similar to Maderian Storm-petrel, but smaller. Generally dark, with a white rump which 'wraps around' the sides of the belly. Tail square-ended, with feet protruding behind. The species feeds by 'walking on the water', forming a V with its wings while paddling with its feet. It generally feeds closer to shore than the other storm-petrels.

DISTRIBUTION: Can be seen following boats close inshore, or feeding near groups of dolphins and killer whales.

BREEDING: Very little is known about the reproduction of this species.

FOOD: Feeds on small fish, crustaceans and 'leftovers' from boats and marine mammals.

WHITE-FACED (FRIGATE) STORM-PETREL *Pelagodroma marina*
Plate p. 41

Sp: Golondrina Cariblanca

STATUS: Vagrant.

IDENTIFICATION: Length 20 cm. Medium-sized storm-petrel, with brownish-grey upperparts, white underparts, pale grey rump and distinctive brown-and-white face-pattern. Seen off San Cristóbal, Santa Cruz and Santiago, and also in the ocean to the southwest of the archipelago.

WHITE-BELLIED STORM-PETREL *Fregetta grallaria* **Plate p. 41**
Sp: Bailarín

STATUS: Vagrant.

IDENTIFICATION: Length 18 cm. Medium-sized storm-petrel, with dark upperparts, tail, head and upper breast, and white rump, underparts and underwing-coverts. Seen southeast of Isabela from May to August, with one specimen seen north of Pinta Island.

WEDGE-RUMPED STORM-PETREL *Oceanodroma tethys tethys*
Plate p. 40

Sp: Golondrina de Tormenta de Galápagos

STATUS: Resident (endemic subspecies).

IDENTIFICATION: Length 19 cm. Mostly dark, with a diagnostic large triangular white patch extending from the rump right down to the base of the tail—far broader than any other storm-petrel. Only the very outer feathers of the tail are dark. This is the only storm-petrel that comes to the breeding-grounds during the day, and feeds by night.

DISTRIBUTION: Can be found near the breeding sites: Pitt Islet (San Cristóbal), Genovesa and probably at Roca Redonda (Isabela). Also seen in the waters between the islands.

BREEDING: Breeds from April to October. Like Maderian Storm-petrel, chooses burrows or natural cavities in the rocks in which to nest. The nest is a simple slight depression. Lays a single white egg, incubated by both parents. Both birds also feed the young.

FOOD: Feeds mainly on fish, squid and crustaceans.

MADEIRAN (BAND-RUMPED) STORM-PETREL
Oceanodroma castro   **Plate p. 40**

Sp: Golondrina de Madeira

STATUS: Resident.

IDENTIFICATION: Length 20 cm, wingspan 44 cm. Mostly black in appearance, with slightly forked tail and narrow white rump band that extends onto upper-tail-coverts. Broad, blunt-ended wings, and buoyant flight with shallow wing-beats and shearwater-like glides. Visits nesting sites during the night.

DISTRIBUTION: Can be found near Cowley (Isabela), Guy Fawkes (Santa Cruz), Caldwell (Floreana), Pitt (San Cristóbal), Plazas, Daphne, Genovesa and Bartolomé islands. However, this bird is an offshore feeder, and may be seen feeding a long way offshore. May also be found in the tropical waters of the Atlantic and Pacific oceans.

BREEDING: In the Galápagos, there are two different populations of this species, which reproduce at different times of the year, although they use the same nesting places. The first group reproduces from February to October, and the second from October to May. Nests in burrows or under rocks, deep enough to hide the bird but still with some light entering. The nest is a small depression on the

Typical nest of Madeiran Storm-petrel

ground where the bird lays a single white egg. Incubation is carried out by both parents and lasts for about 42 days. Once the chick hatches it is fed by both parents for up to 90 days until it is ready to fledge.
FOOD: Likely to feed in deep waters away from land during the day. Appears to feed mainly on squid and small fish.

LEACH'S STORM-PETREL *Oceanodroma leucorhoa*   **Plate p. 41**
Sp: Golondrina de Mar
STATUS: Vagrant.
IDENTIFICATION: Length 21 cm. Largish storm-petrel, with narrow, V-shaped white rump (often with grey central bar), pale upperwing-coverts and bounding flight. Has been reported off Genovesa, Española, Floreana and Wolf.

MARKHAM'S (SOOTY) STORM-PETREL *Oceanodroma markhami*
Plate p. 41
Sp: Golondrina de Markham
STATUS: Vagrant.
IDENTIFICATION: Length 23 cm. Largish, long-winged storm-petrel, all dark except for pale patches on upperwing-coverts. Tail forked. Has been reported off the coasts of Fernandina, and also 100 miles south of the islands. Other reports of 'dark petrels' could include this species.

BLACK STORM-PETREL *Oceanodroma melania*   **Plate p. 41**
Sp: Golondrina de Tormenta Negra
STATUS: Vagrant.
IDENTIFICATION: Length 23 cm, wingspan 46–51 cm. A wholly dark brown storm-petrel, except for a whitish bar on upperwing-coverts. Easily confused with Markham's Storm-petrel, but Black is more energetic in flight, with deeper, stronger wingbeats. Recorded only twice, although common off the coast of Ecuador.

ORDER PELECANIFORMES

This order comprises six families, including the pelicans, boobies, cormorants, frigatebirds, tropicbirds and anhingas. Most are large to medium-sized seabirds, feeding on fish. In the Galápagos, populations of most of the species are stable, with the exception of the endemic Flightless Cormorant, which given its restricted range and low numbers is considered vulnerable.

Family Phaethontidae
Tropicbirds are medium-sized, tropical, pelagic birds with mainly white plumage and two elongated central tail-feathers. They are the only members of this order whose chicks are feathered when hatched.

RED-BILLED TROPICBIRD *Phaethon aethereus*   **Plate p. 35**

Sp: Ave Tropical

STATUS: Resident.

IDENTIFICATION: Length 48 cm, plus tail feathers of 46–56 cm; wingspan 103 cm. Elegant, mainly white bird, with barred grey upperparts, black primaries and black eye-stripe. Bill red, legs yellow. Adults have long central tail feathers (longer in the male), held cocked while swimming. Immature resembles the adult, but the bill is yellow, the dark eye-stripe meets on the nape, and it lacks the elongated tail feathers.

DISTRIBUTION: Found on Santa Cruz, Plazas, Santiago, North Seymour, Daphne and Genovesa where it nests.

BREEDING: Has an unusual breeding cycle: reproduction on Plazas occurring in annual cycles, while on most other islands it occurs throughout the year. This is probably because on Genovesa and the other islands there is so much competition for nesting sites that many pairs fail to reproduce successfully. Failed pairs will restart breeding within a few months, making the breeding season continuous. On Plazas, however, there are plenty of nesting sites, allowing synchronous breeding to occur. The courtship display consists of a beautiful aerial display, accompanied by rattling vocalisations near the nesting area. The nest itself is located in a crevice among the rocks, or just the bare ground. Pairs are faithful to their nest sites. The female lays a single egg, which is incubated by both parents for around 42 days. Both parents feed the young for about 90 days, when it fledges.

FOOD: Feeds pelagically by plunge-diving. The main food items are medium-sized flying-fish, clupeoids (herring-like fish) and squid.

VOICE: A loud rattle produced in flight.

Family Fregatidae

Frigatebirds are large, aerial seabirds which display extraordinary skill in flight, enabling them to parasitise other seabirds. They are the lightest birds in relation to their wingspan. Two species are found in the Galápagos.

MAGNIFICENT FRIGATEBIRD *Fregata magnificens magnificens*
Plate p. 42

Sp: Fragata Real

STATUS: Resident (endemic subspecies).

IDENTIFICATION: Length 89–114 cm, wingspan 217–244 cm. The largest frigatebird, being marginally larger and longer-winged than Great Frigatebird. Rakish, long-winged and long-tailed seabird, with a mainly dark plumage. Male is black, with a purplish sheen on the back and a red gular pouch, which can be inflated like a red balloon during the breeding season. The female is larger than the male, and is completely black except for the breast and shoulders, which are white. The eye-ring is blue. Immatures have white head, neck and breast, changing slowly to black (if male), or the head only goes black (if female). Many birds appear in intermediate plumages. All have a deeply forked tail.

DISTRIBUTION: In the Galápagos, Magnificent Frigatebirds can be found near the coasts of most islands. Breeding colonies are found on Seymour, Gardner Islet, Punta Moreno (Isabela), Wreck Bay and Kicker Rock (San Cristóbal), Daphne Minor, and in mixed colonies with Great Frigatebird on Darwin, Genovesa, Tortuga (Isabela) and Pitt (San Cristóbal).

BREEDING: The male displays its red gular sac to passing females, while calling. The nest is a flimsy arrangement of twigs held together by guano, usually on saltbush or mangroves. One egg is laid. The incubation period is around 50 days, and the feeding of the chick is around 170 days. Both parents are involved in these tasks. Once the chick fledges, the male leaves the nest and will probably breed again. The female continues to take care of the fledgling for another three months or so, until the young bird is ready to fend for itself. In this case the male has a shorter breeding cycle than the female.

FOOD: An inshore feeder, mainly by kleptoparasitism (piracy) on Blue-footed Boobies, or any other passing bird. They also feed on squid, crustaceans and fish waste from fishing boats, sea lion placentae, chicks of most seabirds (including other frigatebirds), and hatchlings of sea turtles and marine iguanas.

VOICE: Male produces a continuous *oo-oo-oo-oo-oo-oo* sound to attract the female.

Frigatebirds mobbing a booby

Magnificent Frigatebird at the nest

GREAT FRIGATEBIRD *Fregata minor ridgwayi*   **Plate p. 42**

Sp: Fragata Común

Status: Resident.

Identification: Length 86–100 cm, wingspan 203–230 cm. Very like Magnificent Frigatebird, though slightly smaller. Male is all black, with a greenish sheen to the back. In the breeding season, has a red gular pouch. The female is all black, apart from the neck and breast which are white. The eye-ring is red or pink. Immature resembles Magnificent but has a rusty shade on the head and breast.

Distribution: Found on Española, Fernandina, Tortuga (Isabela), Genovesa, Punta Pitt (San Cristóbal), Darwin, Wolf and North Seymour (in mixed colony with Magnificent Frigatebird). Rarely seen near the coasts, except on their breeding grounds, as they feed farther out in the ocean.

Breeding: The breeding cycle is very long—lasting nearly two years. It begins with a courtship display, during which the male inflates his bright gular pouch. As a female passes, he vibrates his open wings and calls. This display is performed in clusters of eight or more male birds, which seems very attractive to the females. If a female is interested, she lands and courtship continues to nest-building. The nest is a very poorly designed platform of twigs (often robbed from other nests) and guano. The female lays one egg, which is incubated for about 55 days by both parents. Both also feed the chick for about five months. The period of dependency after fledging is from nine to 12 months. This is for two reasons: first, owing to the species' feeding characteristics, the chick's growth is not steady; and second, because the young bird is not particularly skilful, and if it had to fend for itself it would soon die. During the long dependency period, the juvenile learns the necessary skills to be able to fend for itself.

Food: Great Frigatebird is a pelagic feeder, feeding by picking squid, crustaceans and fish from the water's surface. It also parasitises other seabirds (including its own species), both by stealing food at the moment of feeding, and also by taking unattended chicks. Like Magnificent Frigatebird, it also feeds on sea lion placentae.

Voice: The male gives a continuous rattling call during courtship.

Family Sulidae

Large seabirds with dagger-like bills and wedge-shaped tails. They feed by plunge-diving from a considerable height, and nest in large colonies. The boobies, especially Blue-footed Booby, have elaborate courtship displays.

BLUE-FOOTED BOOBY *Sula nebouxii excisa*   Plate p. 42

Sp: Piquero Patas Azules

Status: Resident (endemic subspecies).

Identification: Length 80 cm, wingspan 152 cm. The middle-sized of the three boobies found in the Galápagos. The best field-mark for the adult is the blue legs and feet (which can vary in colour from lavender through to blue-green). Underparts and part of underwing white. Upperparts mainly brown, apart from white rump and black tail. Head streaked brown and white; bill silvery-grey. The female is larger than the male, and has a pigmented area around the iris that makes the pupil appear larger than that of the male. Immature has grey legs and feet, and a brown head and neck, separated from the wings by a pale stripe.

Distribution: Blue-footed Boobies can be found throughout the archipelago. They breed on all the islands south of the Equator, and have occasionally bred on Genovesa. This species is restricted to the western coasts of tropical America, and the Galápagos holds three-quarters of the world's population.

Breeding: The Blue-footed Booby has an amazing courtship display, involving the very obvious showing of the birds' blue feet to their mates. Breeds opportunistically, with breeding cycles of less than a year. The courtship takes place at the nesting site, which is located on flat areas near the shore. The female lays up to three eggs, which are incubated for around 42 days by both parents. If feeding conditions are favourable they may raise three chicks; if not, siblicide (stronger chick killing the weaker) will occur. Chicks fledge at around 102 days, but the parents continue to feed them for another month and a half until they depart on their own. Immatures leave the islands, and do not return to breed for three or four years.

Food: An inshore feeder. When several birds are feeding in unison they present a real spectacle, in what has been called 'frenzy feeding'. Blue-footed Boobies feed in such shallow waters it is hard to believe that they are not going to collide with the sea-bed. However, they have longer tails than other boobies, which enable them to turn more sharply in the water. Their main prey is fish.

Blue-footed Boobies use their brightly coloured feet in the courtship ritual

MASKED BOOBY *Sula dactylatra granti*   Plate p. 42

Sp: Piquero Enmascarado

STATUS: Resident (endemic subspecies).

IDENTIFICATION: Length 86 cm, wingspan 152 cm. The largest booby found on the islands. Adult completely white, except for black primaries and secondaries and a black tail. Bill, legs and feet yellow. Facial skin is dark, giving 'masked' appearance, hence the name. No difference in coloration between the sexes, though the female is larger and has a duller yellow bill. Immatures have white underparts, with brown head, neck and upperparts (apart from thin white collar).

DISTRIBUTION: Masked Boobies are found throughout the islands. This subspecies also breeds on the islands off Western Mexico.

BREEDING: Masked Booby has a more or less fixed annual breeding cycle, with specific colonies breeding almost at the same time every year. The birds perform a simple courtship, with all the steps of the 'dance' being shorter and less obvious than Blue-footed Booby's. A spot on the ground is chosen for nesting, and a ring of guano can often be observed around the centre of the nest, setting the boundary of the territory. Chicks or eggs that cross this boundary will be abandoned. Two eggs are laid, but only one chick will reach maturity—the extra egg is an 'insurance policy' in case the first is damaged or infertile. If both eggs hatch, the strongest of the siblings (generally the elder one) will kill the other in order to survive. Both parents incubate and feed the chicks.

FOOD: Feeds between the islands, far offshore, for fish.

RED-FOOTED BOOBY *Sula sula websteri* Plate p. 42

Sp: Piquero Patas Rojas

STATUS: Resident (endemic subspecies).

IDENTIFICATION: Length 71 cm, wingspan 96 cm. This is the smallest of the boobies, with several interesting characteristics. It has the largest eyes (the species is semi-nocturnal), it is arboreal, often perching in trees, and lastly it is polymorphic—showing great variation in plumage between individuals. In the Galápagos there are two morphs, one white and one brown, both with black tails (the world's other Red-footed Boobies have white tails). Both have blue, pink and purple facial skin, a blue bill and bright red feet. The white morph is mainly white in plumage, with black primaries and secondaries and a peach-tinted crown. The brown morph (which accounts for 95 per cent of all Red-footed Boobies on the islands) is wholly greyish-brown in colour. Immature resembles the brown morph, but with brown feet and bill.

DISTRIBUTION: Found on San Cristóbal, Genovesa, Wolf, Darwin, Gardner Islet and Marchena, where it nests. Also seen on North Seymour, Isabela and Española. Feeds well off the coast, and can often be sighted when travelling around the waters of the archipelago. The distribution of Red-footed Booby on Galápagos seems to be influenced by the distribution of Galápagos Hawk, its main predator. Red-footed Boobies are present only on islands without Galápagos Hawks.

BREEDING: The breeding cycle lasts for more than a year, and is strongly influenced by the availability of food, and the species' offshore feeding behaviour. The courtship display resembles that of Blue-footed Booby, but is performed on branches of trees near the nesting area.

Plunge-diving boobies

Unlike Red-footed Boobies, which nest in trees, both Blue-footed (above) and Masked Boobies are ground-nesting

The species nests in trees, building a nest from twigs. It lays a single egg, which is incubated by both parents for a period of 45 days. The chick is fed for 130 days, when it fledges, after which there is a further period of food dependency of around 90 days.

Food: Feeds pelagically on fish and squid. Can fish at night.

Family Phalacrocoracidae

Cormorants are diving birds with generally dark plumage and a powerful bill. They dry their wings by holding them open to the wind and sun.

The only representative of this family in the Galápagos is Flightless Cormorant. This species is considered vulnerable, especially given its restricted range and low population level, estimated to be around 800 pairs.

FLIGHTLESS CORMORANT *Nannopterum harrisi*   Plate p. 35

Sp: Cormoran no Volador

Status: Endemic.

Identification: Length 95 cm. Unmistakable: the only cormorant species on the islands, with stubby, useless wings. The adult is brown, lighter along the ventral side, with bright turquoise eyes and a long neck. The male is much larger than the female, and has a darker lower mandible. Immatures are black with brown eyes. The wings, often held open to dry, are extremely short. The birds cannot fly, having lost the keel of the breastbone. When swimming, only the snake-like neck is visible, as the body is kept submerged. Dives from the surface.

Distribution: Flightless Cormorant's range is restricted to the coasts of Fernandina and the western coasts of Isabela, although there are a few colonies on that island's northeastern coast. This distribution coincides with the area of upwelling of rich cold waters from the Humboldt and Cromwell Currents.

BREEDING: It has been estimated that 90 per cent of the clutches are laid between May and October, although there are some discrepancies over laying dates. The birds start their courtship display by performing an aquatic dance, with the routine lasting up to 40 days. The nest is very eleborate, comprising seaweed, dead fish, branches, starfish, sea urchins and any other interesting materials at hand (even including plastic, rope and bottle caps!). It is placed on the rocky shore above the tideline. The male brings presents to the female throughout the incubation period, and she adds them to the nest. She lays up to three eggs which are incubated for about 35 days. If there is plenty of food, the female leaves the male after the incubation and brooding periods and breeds again. The male continues feeding the chicks until they are five to nine months old. This gives the female a breeding cycle of less than a year, while the male's cycle is longer than a year. Flightless Cormorant reproduces when it is two to five years old. It breeds in small colonies, which suggests a great deal of inter-breeding. To maximise the gene flow within the colony, the smallest females choose the largest males, and do not usually breed with the same partner.

FOOD: Feeds within 100 m of the coast, mainly on eels, octopuses and fish. The young are fed by regurgitation. On arrival at the colony, after foraging bouts, the parents wait for up to two hours before feeding the young, presumably to avoid having the food stolen by frigatebirds.

Flightless Cormorant at the nest

81

Family Pelecanidae

Pelicans are highly distinctive, huge birds, with characteristic bills which expand to contain and transport fish. Brown Pelican is the smallest member of the family.

BROWN PELICAN *Pelecanus occidentalis urinator*   **Plate p. 35**

Sp: Pelicano Café

STATUS: Resident (endemic subspecies).

IDENTIFICATION: Length 114 cm, wingspan 203 cm. Huge and unmistakable, with broad wings, heavy body and huge bill. Generally dark brown in colour, though crown, head and neck show extensive pale yellowish shading. In breeding plumage, nape become rusty. Immatures have a grey head and neck.

DISTRIBUTION: This species is found along the coasts of tropical North and South America, but this subspecies nests exclusively in the Galápagos. May be found just offshore on all the islands, often following fishing boats in search of food. It is common to see several birds plunge-diving to feed near the shore.

BREEDING: Little is known about the Brown Pelican's breeding cycle on the islands. They nest in small colonies on all the central islands, and also on Española and Marchena. Breeds throughout the year, with individuals breeding every nine months. The female lays two to three eggs, which are incubated by both parents for around 30 days. The chicks are fed for about 70 days, until they fledge.

FOOD: Feeds on a variety of fish types.

Brown Pelican in the moonlight

ORDER ANSERIFORMES

Family Anatidae

This family includes ducks, geese and swans, collectively known as waterfowl. The main characteristics of this group are their webbed feet, flat bills with tooth-like borders to sieve food, short legs, and slender, pointed wings.

The main representative of this order in the Galápagos is White-cheeked Pintail. Although not considered to be endangered, it may be vulnerable owing to the threats to its habitat.

BLACK-BELLIED WHISTLING-DUCK *Dendrocygna autumnalis*
Plate p. 43

Sp: Guirirí

STATUS: Vagrant.

IDENTIFICATION: Length 50 cm, wingspan 93cm. Medium-sized, colourful duck with rufous upperparts, rufous shading to grey on chest, black belly, grey face and neck, rufous crown and prominent white wing-stripe. The bill is reddish-pink, turning yellow at base. Legs red, white eye-ring. Female similar pattern to male, but duller. Immature brown instead of black, with purplish legs and dark bill. In very young birds the belly is lighter and cross-barred. Very noisy bird, producing a loud whistle.

DISTRIBUTION: Only one record, from a lagoon in southern Isabela. Originates from tropical South America, where common and widespread.

WHITE-CHEEKED PINTAIL *Anas bahamensis galapagensis*
Plate p. 43

Sp: Patillo

STATUS: Resident (endemic subspecies).

IDENTIFICATION: Length 46 cm. Small brown duck with white cheeks and throat, green speculum and black bill with a red triangle at the base. The eyes are bright red. Chicks are yellow with brown markings.

DISTRIBUTION: This subspecies is restricted to the Galápagos, where it is commonly found on all the lagoons and temporary pools, both along the shoreline and in the highlands of all the large islands. It can also be found on Genovesa, Rábida, Pinzón, Santa Fé, Seymour and Española if rains are plentiful.

BREEDING: Nests in thick vegetation on the ground near the lagoons' shore. Has been reported breeding in January, March, May and July. It is possible that nesting occurs from January to May both along the coast and in the highlands, and from June to December in the highlands if there is enough rain. If this is the case, the bird could be described as an opportunistic breeder. Up to ten brown eggs are laid, and are incubated by the female for around 25 days. Once hatched, the chicks can swim and feed on their own.

FOOD: Feeds in shallow waters by submerging half its body, leaving only the tail on the surface. Although a dabbling duck, it is very common to observe this species diving for food in the deeper freshwater lagoons of San Cristóbal. Feeds on water plants.

VOICE: Males whistle, females make honking sounds.

BLUE-WINGED TEAL *Anas discors*   Plate p. 43

Sp: Cerceta Aliazul

STATUS: Vagrant.

IDENTIFICATION: Length 39 cm, wingspan 63cm. A small, attractive duck. Adult mainly brown, spotted with black. Head and neck of adult male bluish-grey, with white crescent marking extending from just above eye to base of head. Female has pale buff, unspotted head. Male and female have pale powder-blue wing-coverts and green speculum. In flight, blue on wing distinctive. Male has whistling call.

DISTRIBUTION: A vagrant from North America. Has been reported from lagoons on Isabela, Santa Cruz and San Cristóbal. Also reported from the highlands of Santa Cruz. Dates of sightings range from December to April.

ORDER PHOENICOPTERIFORMES

Family Phoenicopteridae

Flamingos are large wading birds, with long legs and neck, webbed feet and a distinctive large, chunky bill, with a sharp downward kink at its midway point. The characteristic bill contains a series of sieve-like plates which the birds use to filter food from the brackish waters where they usually live.

One species, Greater Flamingo, is found on the islands, where it is considered to be vulnerable. Its population is around 500 to 700 birds, with an annual mortality amongst adults of around 10 per cent, and for immatures as high as 30 per cent.

GREATER FLAMINGO *Phoenicopterus ruber*   Plate p. 43

Sp: Flamenco

STATUS: Resident.

IDENTIFICATION: Length 105 cm, wingspan 138 cm. Unmistakable. Adult is conspicuously peach-coloured, with contrasting black primaries. The distal half of the bill and the eyes are strikingly yellow. Males are slightly larger than females, although this is of little use in the field unless the birds are performing their courtship dance. During this dance their necks are stretched, making the size difference readily apparent. They fly with legs and neck extended, with the black primaries clearly visible. The downy chick is white, turning greyish after a few days. The juvenile is white. Hatchlings have black, straight bills that curve after three weeks.

DISTRIBUTION: Found in saltwater lagoons on the islands of Floreana, Santa Cruz, Isabela, Santiago and Rábida, and on Bainbridge Rocks. The species can also be seen in flight while migrating between lagoons or islands.

BREEDING: Greater Flamingo has a lifespan of some 15 to 30 years, breeding for the first time at about five years of age. It generally nests once a year, but a given bird does not necessarily nest every year. The breeding season runs from July to March. Although still not known for certain, scientists believe that the nesting lagoons are mainly selected on the basis of water level. Depending on the availability of food, breeding birds may have to feed in lagoons away from the nesting site. If conditions are not favourable, flamingos may not nest at all. The flamingos of the Galápagos are the only ones of this colonial species that nest in groups of fewer than ten birds. The breeding season starts with an intricate courtship dance, accompanied by sounds from all the birds in the group. After mating, the female selects a place to build a castle-like nest out of mud, where she lays a single white egg. Incubation is shared by both parents, and lasts from 28 to 30 days. The chick leaves the nest and joins other youngsters in creches when it is about 11 days old. It is fed by both parents for up to three-and-a-half months, after which time it is able to feed on its own and fly. The fledged juvenile then leaves the lagoon for better feeding areas elsewhere.

FOOD: Feeds mainly on water boatmen (*Trichocorixia reticulata*) and shrimps (*Artemia salina*).

VOICE: A series of *uh-uh-uh, ah-ah-ah* calls.

Greater Flamingo nests

ORDER CICONIIFORMES

Family Ardeidae

Herons and egrets are wading birds with long, thin legs, a long neck, and long, straight bills. Flight is slow, with the head often held hunched back towards the shoulders. During the mating season they display beautiful long feathers, called aigrettes or plumes. They are usually silent, emitting only infrequent alarm calls.

Herons and egrets are not considered endangered species in the archipelago, although little is known about their ecology there.

SNOWY EGRET *Leucophoyx thula*   Plate p. 44

Sp: Garcita Blanca

STATUS: Migrant.

IDENTIFICATION: Length 61 cm, wingspan 104 cm. Slightly larger and more elegant than Cattle Egret, with a totally white plumage. Adult has long white plumes on head, neck and breast. Bright yellow feet and black legs and bill.

DISTRIBUTION: Reported from Santa Cruz, southern Isabela and Punta Cormorant, and Floreana.

GREAT BLUE HERON *Ardea herodias*   Plate p. 45

Sp: Garza Morena

STATUS: Resident.

IDENTIFICATION: Length 95 cm, wingspan 175 cm. This is the largest heron in the Galápagos. Sexes alike. Upperparts uniform pale grey-blue (lighter than its continental counterparts). Head white with a black stripe on the sides and rear of crown. Underparts white, with the breast spotted black, and pale cinnamon 'thighs'. During the mating periods, shows aigrettes on the back of the head, chest and back. The legs and bill are yellowish. The white phase of this species is not found in the archipelago.

DISTRIBUTION: Found in the intertidal zones, among the mangroves and in the saltwater lagoons of Isabela, San Cristóbal, Santa Cruz, Fernandina, Santiago and Floreana. Rare on Española and Genovesa. Not reported from Marchena, Pinta, Wolf and Darwin.

BREEDING: Reproduction occurs throughout the year. The large nest is built either on high branches of trees such as mangroves, or on rocks by cliffs. The nest comprises twigs and branches, and is often used more than once. Great Blue Heron is a solitary breeder, but may share the nesting area with other birds. The clutch size is two or three eggs, incubated for about 28 days by both parents. The chicks are fed by both parents.

FOOD: The principal food is small fish obtained from intertidal pools or near the shore. Less frequent food sources include lava lizards and young marine iguanas and turtles. The young feed on regurgitated food.

VOICE: The alarm call is a series of hoarse squawks.

Great Blue Heron at Puerto Ayora dock

GREAT EGRET *Casmerodius albus*   **Plate p. 44**

Sp: Garza Blanca

STATUS: Resident.

IDENTIFICATION: Length 80 cm, wingspan 138 cm. Large, elegant heron, second only in size to Great Blue Heron. Sexes alike. Plumage completely white, bill and legs yellow, feet black. In breeding plumage displays long scapular aigrettes.

DISTRIBUTION: Can be found around lagoons, in the intertidal zone and in the grassy areas of the highlands on Isabela, Fernandina, Santa Cruz, San Cristóbal and Floreana. Not known from the northern islands of Pinta, Marchena, Wolf and Darwin. Not so common as Great Blue Heron.

BREEDING: Breeds in colonies. Nests are built near the shore on mangroves. The most usual clutch size in the Galápagos is two eggs.

FOOD: Feeds on small fish and insects.

VOICE: A harsh *cawca* or rasping *ca-aa-auw*.

CATTLE EGRET *Bubulcus ibis*   **Plate p. 44**

Sp: Garza (del Ganado) Bueyera

STATUS: Resident.

IDENTIFICATION: Length 51 cm, wingspan 91 cm. Medium-sized, short-necked heron, much smaller and more compact than Great Egret. Sexes alike. At distance appears all-white, but in breeding season the feathers on the crown,

yellow bill, and black legs and feet.

DISTRIBUTION: Found in large numbers in the agricultural zones of Isabela, San Cristóbal, Santa Cruz and Floreana, although individuals can be found near the shore on lava rocks, amongst the mangroves, or in the lagoon areas of most islands. The Cattle Egret comes originally from Africa, but its characteristic association with cattle has permitted the species to become virtually cosmopolitan. The presence of cattle farms on the inhabited islands is probably the reason for its establishment on the Galápagos, since it was first recorded in 1964.

BREEDING: Until 1986 it was considered a migrant, but is now known to breed at Tercera Playa on Isabela, and Tortuga and Conway Bays on Santa Cruz. Cattle Egret has been reported in breeding plumage in both seasons, so breeding probably occurs throughout the year. The species nests in colonies, laying two or three eggs.

FOOD: Feeds on insects disturbed by cattle, sea lions and tortoises during their daily activities.

VOICE: When at the nest emits a *rick-rack* noise, and a harsh *roo* and muffled *thunk* during courtship.

STRIATED HERON *Butorides striatus*   **Plate p. 45**

Sp: Garza Verde

STATUS: Resident.

IDENTIFICATION: Length 35 cm, wingspan 63 cm. Similar in size and shape to Lava Heron. Upperparts: uniform dark green except for black crown. Underparts: neck and breast cream with green-brown striations. Bill and legs silver-grey. In breeding plumage the legs turn orange and the male's bill black. Immature resembles young Lava Heron: greenish brown above and heavily streaked brown below, with yellow legs and black bill.

DISTRIBUTION: Has been reported nesting on Isabela, Santa Cruz, Fernandina, Pinzón and Pinta.

BREEDING and FOOD: Behaviour resembles that of Lava Heron.

VOICE: As Lava Heron.

LAVA HERON *Butorides sundevalli*   **Plate p. 45**

Sp: Garza de Lava

STATUS: Endemic.

IDENTIFICATION: Length 35 cm, wingspan 63 cm. A very small, compact heron. Adult has ash-grey underparts and upperparts, very similar in colour to lava. It has been suggested that this colour was favoured from an evolutionary point of view as a means of enabling the heron to hide from predatory frigatebirds. In non-breeding plumage, the legs are grey and the bill is silver-grey, while in breeding plumage the legs become orange and the male's bill turns shiny black. Can be confused with Striated Heron, but Lava Heron lacks black crown and striations on the chest typical of that species. The immature's upperparts are greenish-brown; underparts cream, heavily spotted with brown. Legs yellow, bill silver-grey.

DISTRIBUTION: Found in the intertidal zone and among the mangroves on the coasts of all the islands. Also a common sight on the saltwater lagoons.

BREEDING: Activity starts soon after the first heavy rains. Nests under rocks or among the lower branches of mangroves, both on the coast and around the lagoons. This species is a solitary nester, and is very territorial, protecting relatively small areas. Lays two or three eggs. If the conditions are favourable can nest up to three times per year.

FOOD: Feeds on small fish found in the intertidal pools and along the edge of the lagoons. Also feeds on lava lizards, crabs and insects.

VOICE: The alarm call is a sharp *keoup*. The easiest way to find out if an immature heron is in the area is to listen for the adults' alarm call as you approach.

YELLOW-CROWNED NIGHT HERON *Nyctanassa violacea pauper*
Plate p. 45

Sp: Guaque, or Garza Nocturna
STATUS: Resident (endemic subspecies).
IDENTIFICATION: Length 61 cm, wingspan 107 cm. A medium-sized, plump, squat-looking heron. Sexes alike. Upperparts and underparts bluish-grey. Head darker than the rest of the body, showing a yellow crown and a distinctive white mark on the cheeks. When alarmed two yellow aigrettes rise from the crown. Upperwings dark bluish-grey, with white spotting. Legs yellow, and the bill is thick and black. Immature has entire body brown-spotted, with dull greenish beak and legs. When seen in flight, the legs protrude beyond the tail.
DISTRIBUTION: During the day, can be found along the coasts, on rocks or in the mangroves. Found on all the islands except Wolf and Darwin. However, the species is easier to observe at dusk on the populated islands, flying towards its feeding grounds and feeding underneath street lamps. It has been seen in large flocks around the lagoon at the Genovesa tourist trail at dusk.
BREEDING: Nests throughout the year in nests made of twigs between mangrove roots or under rocks. Lays three or four eggs, incubated by both parents.

Yellow-crowned Night Heron hunting

Food: On the uninhabited islands feeds on crustaceans and insects, while on the populated islands feeds mainly on insects and other invertebrates attracted by street lights, such as beetles, locusts, centipedes, scorpions and cockroaches.
Voice: *Quck* or *quok*. This nocturnal alarm call often scares visitors.

BLACK-CROWNED NIGHT HERON *Nycticorax nycticorax*
Plate p. 45

Sp: Garza Nocturna
Status: Vagrant.
Identification: Length 64 cm, wingspan 112 cm. Similar shape and build as previous species. Upperparts: crown and back black; neck, wings, rump and tail grey. Underparts: greyish-white. Legs yellow, bill black.
Distribution: A single record of a subadult bird found at Tortuga Bay, Santa Cruz, in 1971.

ORDER FALCONIFORMES

Members of this order have hooked bills and strong, curved, powerful talons that enable them to take their prey alive. However, they can also be scavengers. Females are generally larger than males.

The only resident member of this order in the Galápagos is the endemic Galápagos Hawk. This species is regarded as rare in the ICBP *Red Data Book*. It is believed that its population was very high before colonisation began, but that during the first two years of colonisation 15,000 birds were killed on Santa Cruz alone. Today the population on this island is down to only two pairs, with the total Galápagos population estimated in 1970 at between 130 and 150 pairs. No census has been carried out recently.

Family Pandionidae

OSPREY *Pandion haliaetus*
Plate p. 46

Sp: Aguila Pescadora
Status: Migrant.
Identification: Length 55–69 cm; wingspan 145–160 cm. Given good views, unmistakable. A large, long-winged raptor, showing generally dark upperparts contrasting with pale underparts, and white head. In flight, shows a conspicuous crook in its wings, which are often held in an arched position, and black 'wrists' and wingtips. While flying at low altitiudes it usually flaps its wings. When perched, the dark wings and back contrasting with the pale underparts and dark mask across the eyes are very distinctive. Often seen plunge-diving for its staple food, fish, which it lifts out of the water with its sharp talons.
Distribution: Has been seen on Isabela, Fernandina, San Cristóbal and Santa Cruz between June and January.

Family Accipitridae

GALÁPAGOS HAWK *Buteo galapagoensis* **Plate p. 46**
Sp: Gavilán de Galápagos
Status: Endemic.
Identification: Length 56 cm, wingspan 120 cm. Adult uniformly dark brown, with lighter patches on the shoulders, and paler primaries and secondaries in flight. Bill pale, with dark tip and yellow at base; legs and feet yellow. Female larger than male. Immature paler, especially around head and neck, with mottled yellowish-brown underparts. The newly hatched chicks are snowy white, turning dirty white soon afterwards.
Distribution: Present on almost all the islands, with the exception of Genovesa, Wolf, Darwin, San Cristóbal, Baltra, Seymour, Daphne and Floreana (recently eradicated by humans). Can be found both in the highlands and lowlands, but nesting is restricted to the lowlands.
Breeding: This hawk has a very unusual and interesting mating system. Up to four males pair with a single female, helping to protect a common territory and carrying on incubation and feeding of the young. This system, called coopera-tive polyandry, increases the chances of breeding success for each individual

A giant tortoise makes a ready-made perch for this Galápagos Hawk

involved. Each territory is between 0.5 and 2 km² in size, and is protected even outside the breeding season. Breeding occurs in all months, with the peak in June and July. It starts with an aerial display that is both a signal to neighbouring hawks to keep out of the territory, and part of the birds' courtship. During this flight the male flies above the female diving towards her from time to time. As he approaches she turns towards him showing her claws. After some time she lands and mating takes place, with each male in the group mating with the female one after another. Copulation takes place several times a day. As with many species, they build more than one nest per territory, but only use one per season. Nests are built on trees or rocky outcrops, so the birds are able to watch over their territory. The nests grow larger from year to year, with more twigs and leaves added each time the nest is reused. Two or three eggs are laid and incubation lasts about 40 days. Although all the polyandrous males help, the female does most of the incubation. Chicks fledge after 50 to 60 days. Parents expel the young birds from their territories three to five months after fledging. Immature birds spend the next two years in non-territorial areas, before establishing themselves in old territories or forming their own to breed.

Food: Galápagos Hawk is both a predator and a scavenger, feeding on a great range of foods. Young marine iguanas, sea turtles, boobies, adult landbirds, introduced and native rats are all live prey. It also feeds on the placentae of sea lions, and the carcasses of goats and other animals.

Voice: The hawk has several calls, including *klee, klee, klee, klee; kleeuu, kleeuu, kleeuu, kleeuu,* and *chick, chick, chick.*

Family Falconidae

These birds are excellent, strong fliers with pointed wings and a long slender tail.

PEREGRINE FALCON *Falco peregrinus*   Plate p. 46

Sp: Alcón Peregrino

Status: Migrant.

Identification: Length 39–50 cm; wingspan 95–115 cm. A fast-flying, powerfully built falcon, always giving the impression of strength and vigour. Female usually larger than male. Upperparts steel-grey, with paler base of tail and rump. Underparts pale, but heavily barred with dark grey, especially on the belly. Throat paler, contrasting with dark face and head, and conspicuous moustachial stripes. In flight appears all dark above, paler below, with deep chest and broad-based wings. When attacking prey can reach tremendous speeds while 'stooping' from a great height. Immatures are browner, with heavier spotting rather than barring on the underparts.

Distribution: Has been seen on the islands of Baltra, Isabela, Santa Cruz, Española and Plazas, mainly from November to March, but a couple of records are from May and June.

ORDER GRUIFORMES

Family Rallidae

Rails and crakes are secretive wading birds, usually found on the edges of fresh-water areas and in marshes. Some species are very elusive, and many are crepuscular, emerging mainly at dawn and dusk to feed.

All members of this family in the Galápagos are potentially endangered, since their habitat is a vulnerable one. Special efforts in particular should be made to study the endemic Galápagos Crake, to determine its status and establish a viable management plan.

GALÁPAGOS CRAKE *Laterallus spilonotus*   Plate p. 34

Sp: Pachay

STATUS: Endemic.
IDENTIFICATION: Length 15 cm. A tiny, chocolate-brown rail, with a chestnut back speckled with white, and bright red eyes. Spends most of the time running through 'runways' in the vegetation. Once a runway is found it is possible to attract the bird by clapping hands. Immatures are paler than adults, and lack the white spots on the back.
DISTRIBUTION: Originally inhabited the mangrove zone and the highlands of Santiago, Isabela, Santa Cruz, San Cristóbal, Pinta, Fernandina and Floreana. The species appears to be declining, being no longer found in the lowlands of any of the islands. It has not been reported from Floreana since 1983, and it is now very rare on San Cristóbal where it was once abundant.
BREEDING: Occurs from June to February. The nest, made on the ground, has a lateral entrance and is covered with dense, low vegetation. Lays up to five eggs. Both parents incubate, for a period of between 23 and 25 days. Young birds reach maturity after around 80 days.
FOOD: Invertebrates and seeds.

SORA RAIL *Porzana carolina*   Plate p. 34

Sp: Polluela Norteña

STATUS: Vagrant.
IDENTIFICATION: Length 22 cm. A small, brownish-olive rail, back is coarsely black-streaked, with fine white feather edges. Bill is yellow or greenish-yellow. Breeding adults have black throat and face, fading browner in non-breeding plumage. Immature is paler and browner, with more heavily streaked back. Found in similar lowland habitat to Galápagos Crake.
DISTRIBUTION: Three records, all of dead birds, on Marchena, James and Tower.

PAINT-BILLED CRAKE *Neocrex erythrops*   Plate p. 34

Sp: Gallareta

STATUS: Resident.
IDENTIFICATION: Length 20 cm. A small, dark rail, fairly secretive in its habits.

Underparts and upperparts dark greyish. The bill is red and yellow, while the legs are red.

DISTRIBUTION: Found in the farm zones of Santa Cruz, Isabela, Floreana and San Cristóbal. A specimen was found alive on Genovesa in 1986, and another dead bird was found on Rábida in 1989. On Santa Cruz the species has been found in the lowlands.

BREEDING: Probably reproduces from December to May. The cup-shaped nest is built on the ground, hidden by vegetation. Lays six or seven eggs which hatch after about twenty days. The chicks are ready to leave the nest immediately after hatching, and follow the female in search of food.

FOOD: Feeds on small invertebrates.

PURPLE GALLINULE *Porphyrula martinica*   **Plate p. 34**

Sp: Gallito Azul

STATUS: Vagrant.

IDENTIFICATION: Length 33 cm, wingspan 52 cm. Distinctive, medium-sized rail, with glossy purple and green plumage. Head, neck and underparts glossy purple, olive-brown back and greenish wings. Blue frontal shield, red bill with yellow tip. Legs yellow-olive. Undertail white. Immatures are paler, with a brownish-olive back and pale buffish underparts, dark olive bill and olive legs.

DISTRIBUTION: Vagrant from North, Central or South America. Has been reported from Santa Cruz (a dead specimen), El Junco and La Toma (San Cristóbal), and Punta Suarez (Española), where it was photographed alive.

COMMON GALLINULE (MOORHEN) *Gallinula chloropus*
     Plate p. 34

Sp: Gallinula

STATUS: Resident.

IDENTIFICATION: Length 34 cm, wingspan 52 cm. A medium-sized, duck-like waterbird. Adults slaty-black, with a bright red frontal shield on the forehead, and red bill with a yellow tip. Broken white stripe along flanks. The undertail is white, and flashes while the bird is swimming or walking through vegetation. Immature paler and browner, with a dark bill and no frontal plate. When swimming the head moves back and forth in a very distinctive, jerky manner.

DISTRIBUTION: Can be found on the freshwater lagoon of El Junco and the water reservoir of La Toma on San Cristóbal. Also found on the brackish water lagoons of southern Isabela, Santa Cruz, San Cristóbal, Floreana and possibly Fernandina.

BREEDING: Probably reproduces from May to October. The nests are built near the shore of the lagoons. The only nest that has been reported contained seven eggs.

FOOD: Feeds on vegetable matter and invertebrates living near the shore, or on the water's surface.

VOICE: A variety of sharp *kik* and *kek* calls.

ORDER CHARADRIIFORMES

This group includes a broad range of wading and swimming birds, such as waders, gulls, terns and auks. Most are found near coasts, feeding and breeding on or near the shoreline, although many species also spend part of the year inland. Most representatives of this order found in the Galápagos are migratory species which are overwintering in the islands. However, a few species have found suitable niches, and breed there.

Family Scolopacidae

MARBLED GODWIT *Limosa fedoa*   Plate p. 47
Sp: Aguja Canela
Status: Vagrant.
Identification: Length 46 cm. Large, brown wader with long legs, neck and distinctive long, slightly upcurved bill. Overall appearance more like a curlew than a godwit. Upperparts mid-brown, speckled with blackish and cinnamon. Underparts buffy cinnamon colour, lightly streaked with black on upper chest and flanks. Bill long, and slightly upcurved, usually orange-brown at base and centre and black towards tip. Head-pattern shows dark crown and cheeks contrasting with pale supercilium and dark lores. In flight, appears mainly cinnamon-buff, with darker primaries, and bright cinnamon on underwings.
Distribution: Has been seen on Santa Cruz, Isabela (Villamil) and San Cristóbal, usually from October to March.
Voice: Contact calls are a loud and harsh *cor-ack*; also gives a sharp *wik-wik* in alarm.

WHIMBREL *Numenius phaeopus hudsonicus*   Plate p. 48
Sp: Zarapito
Status: Migrant.
Identification: Length 45 cm. Large, mainly brown wader, with distinctive downcurved bill. Upperparts dark brown, with paler spots and fringes to the feathers. Underparts pale buff, heavily streaked with dark brown, shading to white on lower belly and undertail. Head pattern distinctive, with pale crown stripe, dark sides to crown, pale supercilium and dark eye-stripe. Bill shortish and downcurved. In flight shows dark wings, rump and tail.
Distribution: Can be found feeding on lagoons where the birds also congregate to roost (on Quinta Playa lagoon, Isabela, more than 700 birds have been seen at dusk). Also seen in the highlands, where birds feed around temporary freshwater pools. Can be seen all year round in large numbers.
Voice: A series of rippling notes, evenly emphasised on the same tone.

GREATER YELLOWLEGS *Tringa melanoleuca*   **Plate p. 48**

Sp: Chorlo Real

STATUS: Rare migrant.

IDENTIFICATION: Length 36 cm. A large, long-legged and long-billed wader, superficially similar to Lesser Yellowlegs, but can usually be told apart fairly easily. Overall appearance larger and bulkier than Lesser. As with Lesser, head and upperparts mainly grey, speckled with white; and underparts white, streaked with grey on chest and flanks. Bill longer and stouter than Lesser, often tilting fractionally upwards. Legs long and orange-yellow. In flight also shows square white patch on uppertail coverts, contrasting with dark wings; legs projecting beyond tail.

DISTRIBUTION: Has been reported from lagoons on Santiago, Isabela, Santa Cruz and Floreana.

VOICE: A sharp three to five note whistle: *tew-tew-tew-tew*.

LESSER YELLOWLEGS *Tringa flavipes*   **Plate p. 48**

Sp: Chorlo Chico

STATUS: Migrant.

IDENTIFICATION: Length 27 cm. Slim, elegant, medium-sized wader with longish neck and legs. Head, mantle, neck, back and wings are grey, speckled with white. Underparts mainly white, with grey streaks on upper chest and flanks. Throat white. Bill straight, slim and pointed. Legs (the best fieldmark) are bright orange-yellow. On the ground the wings project noticeably beyond the tail. In flight shows neat, square white patch on uppertail-coverts, contrasting with dark wings, back and tail; legs projecting beyond tip of tail.

DISTRIBUTION: Has been seen frequently along the shores of fresh and saltwater lagoons on Isabela, Floreana, Santa Cruz and Genovesa. Has also been reported from the highlands of San Cristóbal. Occurs from October to March.

FOOD: Feeds on invertebrates and other morsels, often picked off the water's surface with a delicate, deliberate feeding action.

VOICE: A whistled *tew* or *tew-tew*—a useful distinction from the longer call of Greater Yellowlegs.

SOLITARY SANDPIPER *Tringa solitaria*   **Plate p. 47**

Sp: Playero Solitario

STATUS: Migrant.

IDENTIFICATION: Length 22 cm. A medium-sized wader with contrasting dark above, white below. Head, neck, upper chest and upperparts very dark olive-green, spotted with white, but appearing almost black at a distance. Belly and undertail white. Legs dull green, bill dark, short and straight. In flight appears all dark above, including rump and tail.

DISTRIBUTION: Seen in the highlands of Santa Cruz and San Cristóbal during the northern hemisphere winter months (December–February).

VOICE: A mixture of high-pitched *tou-tou-twit* and single *tew* and *pit* calls.

SPOTTED SANDPIPER *Actitis macularia*   **Plate p. 49**

Sp: Correlino
STATUS: Migrant.
IDENTIFICATION: Length 19 cm. Small, plumpish, dark wader. In summer plumage has distinctively spotted underparts which give the species its name. In winter underparts are white and unmarked, apart from a greyish-green patch on the sides of the upper breast. Head and upperparts darker olive-green, with faint streaking on wing-feathers. Bill short, straight and dark; legs pinkish-yellow. Distinctive 'bobbing' gait, holding its body forward while wagging its short tail up and down.
DISTRIBUTION: Winter visitor (northern hemisphere). Most common on Santa Cruz, although it has also been reported from Floreana, Marchena and Isabela.
VOICE: Flight call is thin and piping, a series of *peet* notes, descending in pitch towards the end.

WANDERING TATTLER *Heteroscelus incanum*   **Plate p. 49**

Sp: Errante
STATUS: Migrant.
IDENTIFICATION: Length 28 cm. One of the commonest migratory coastal birds found in the archipelago. Usually seen alone, but also found in pairs. In non-breeding plumage appears mainly grey, with plain, dark grey upperparts, paler grey underparts, and a white belly. Legs yellow, bill long, pointed and dark. In breeding plumage underparts and belly heavily barred with grey.
DISTRIBUTION: Found on the coasts of all the islands, throughout the year.
VOICE: Rapid burst of peeping whistles, all at the same pitch. Frequently heard.

WILLET *Catoptrophorus semipalmatus*   **Plate p. 49**

Sp: Playero Aliblanco
STATUS: Migrant.
IDENTIFICATION: Length 38 cm. A large, slender, long-legged wader. Upperparts greyish-brown, with pale feather edgings giving mottled effect. Underparts pale grey, shading to white on belly and undertail. Best recognised in flight, by its distinctive black-and-white striped wing pattern. Bill short and dark, legs long and grey. Rump white, tail greyish.
DISTRIBUTION: Reported from Isabela, Pinta, Floreana, Santiago and Santa Cruz during the northern hemisphere winter months.
VOICE: A noisy wader, with loud *kip* alarm, and characteristic *pill-will-willet* calls, from which the bird takes its name.

RUDDY TURNSTONE *Arenaria interpres*   **Plate p. 50**

Sp: Vuelve Piedras
STATUS: Migrant.
IDENTIFICATION: Length 24 cm. A medium-sized, short-legged wader, generally found on shorelines. In summer plumage very colourful, with white head,

throat and underparts contrasting with black facial markings and breast band, and rufous and black upperparts. Bill short and black, legs short and red. In flight shows strongly marked wings, with broad stripes of rufous, black and white. In winter plumage much duller, with brown and black upperparts, neck and chest contrasting with white belly. Immatures have darker upperparts than adults with no rusty colour.

DISTRIBUTION: Commonly found along the coasts of Santa Cruz, Isabela, Genovesa, Española and also feeds on the saltwater lagoons of Isabela and Santa Cruz. May be seen throughout the year.

FOOD: The species gets its name from its habit of turning over stones, shells and other objects to find food. Diet consists mainly of small molluscs, insects and their larvae, and crustaceans.

VOICE: Low-pitched, throaty rattle, clear and quick, *trik-tuk-tuk-tuk*.

BLACK TURNSTONE *Arenaria melanocephala*   Plate p. 50

Sp: Vuelvepiedras Negro

STATUS: Vagrant.

IDENTIFICATION: Length 24 cm. Similar in shape and general appearance to previous species. In non-breeding plumage appears very dark above, contrasting with white belly. Head, chest and upperparts dark brown to black, apart from short white patch on wing. Belly and undertail white. Dark legs and bill. In flight shows white wing-bars and rump, and white outer tail feathers contrasting with dark centre to tail.

DISTRIBUTION: Has been reported once from the highlands of San Cristóbal.

VOICE: Similar to Ruddy Turnstone, but higher-pitched and less staccato.

SHORT-BILLED DOWITCHER *Limnodromus griseus*   Plate p. 49

Sp: Agujeta Piquicorta

STATUS: Migrant.

IDENTIFICATION: Length 28 cm. A bulky, medium-sized wader with a long, straight bill. Upperparts brownish-grey, with pale fringes to the feathers. Underparts greyish-white, with light streaking on chest and barred flanks. Head grey, with prominent pale supercilium. Bill long, straight and black; legs olive-yellow. In flight shows white triangular patch from centre of back to rump. Tail barred with black.

DISTRIBUTION: Has been reported from Floreana, Isabela, San Cristóbal and Santiago, and may be a regular non-breeding visitor.

VOICE: Resembles Ruddy Turnstone, a rapid *tu-tu-tu*.

SURFBIRD *Aphriza virgata*   Plate p. 49

Sp: Chorlito de Rompientes

STATUS: Migrant.

IDENTIFICATION: Length 25 cm. Medium-sized, plump wader, similar in size and shape to Turnstone. In winter plumage mainly dark grey, apart from small white patch on throat and whitish belly and undertail. Flanks streaked with grey. Bill short and dark, with yellowish base. In flight shows white rump contrasting with dark tail, and white wing-bars.

DISTRIBUTION: Reported during the northern hemisphere winter months from Santiago, Plazas, Isabela and Santa Cruz.

VOICE: Usually silent, but sometimes produces a melancholy, plaintive whistle.

RED KNOT *Calidris canutus*   Plate p. 47

Sp: Playero Pecho Rufo

STATUS: Vagrant.

IDENTIFICATION: Length 27 cm. A medium-sized, chunky-looking wader, with very contrasting summer and winter plumages. In summer, underparts, throat and face are bright brick-red, with black, brown, grey and orange upperparts. Short, straight dark bill, greenish legs. In winter mainly grey above, with whitish fringes to feathers; pale below, with variable grey streaking on upper chest and flanks. Always looks plump and short-legged. In flight shows distinctive white rump, contrasting with dark wings and tail.

DISTRIBUTION: A single bird was reported from Punta Cormorant (Floreana) in 1969.

VOICE: Not particularly vocal, a single, infrequent *knutt* call sometimes made.

Roosting Red Knot

SANDERLING *Calidris alba*   Plate p. 47

Sp: Playero Común

STATUS: Migrant.

IDENTIFICATION: Length 20 cm. Small, compact wader, best identified by its habit of running rapidly along the tideline like a clockwork toy. In winter plumage very pale, with pearl-grey crown and upperparts and white underparts. Legs short and dark; bill short, straight and dark. In flight shows darker edges to

Sanderlings at Villamil

wings, contrasting with strong white wing-bar, and very white underwing.
DISTRIBUTION: Has been reported from all islands with the exception of Pinzón, Genovesa, Wolf and Darwin. None of these islands has beaches, which probably explains the species' absence. Generally found along beaches or on the edges of the salt lagoons. Can be seen throughout the year.
VOICE: Gives a quiet *kip* or *wik* in flight.

SEMIPALMATED SANDPIPER *Calidris pusilla*   Plate p. 50
Sp: Playero Semipalmeado
STATUS: Vagrant.
IDENTIFICATION: Length 16 cm. Small sandpiper, easily confused with Least. Best told apart by black legs (yellow in Least's). Quite stout, straight bill, thicker at base than tip.
DISTRIBUTION: Has been reported from Isabela, Floreana and Santa Cruz during the northern hemisphere winter months.
VOICE: Normal calls are low-pitched and coarse, including a loud *cherk* or *chrup.*

WESTERN SANDPIPER *Calidris mauri*   Plate p. 50
Sp: Playero Occipital
STATUS: Vagrant.
IDENTIFICATION: Length 17 cm. In winter plumage, very similar to Semipalmated Sandpiper, apart from slightly longer, more downcurved bill.
DISTRIBUTION: Has been seen on Santiago, Santa Fé and Floreana during the northern hemisphere winter months.
VOICE: High-pitched, thin and sharp *cheet* calls are given in flight.

LEAST SANDPIPER *Calidris minutilla*   **Plate p. 47**

Sp: Playero Enano
STATUS: Migrant.
IDENTIFICATION: Length 15 cm. Tiny shorebird, together with Semipalmated Sandpiper the smallest found in the Galápagos. Upperparts dull brown, sometimes showing pale feather edges and faint stripes down back. Underparts whitish, with dark streaks on upper chest. Legs most useful distinguishing feature, being yellowish or greenish, rather than dark as in the case of Semipalmated. Bill short, dark and slightly downcurved.
DISTRIBUTION: Can be found along the shoreline, or at the pool margins and sandy beaches of the saline lagoons on Floreana, San Cristóbal, Santa Cruz and Santiago. Present throughout the year, but in largest numbers from October to April.
VOICE: Usual calls are high-pitched and shrill, sometimes rendered as *trree.*

WHITE-RUMPED SANDPIPER *Calidris fuscicollis*   **Plate p. 50**

Sp: Playero de Rabadilla Blanca
STATUS: Vagrant.
IDENTIFICATION: Length 19 cm. A smallish, grey-looking wader with distinctively long wings. Upperparts dark grey, scalloped with black; head, neck and upper chest paler grey, with white supercilium and throat. Belly and undertail white. Legs short and dark; bill short, dark and slightly downcurved. At rest, wings project beyond tip of tail. In flight shows distinctive white rump, contrasing with dark wings and tail.
DISTRIBUTION: One bird has been seen at Cabo Hammond (Fernandina), and two were photographed at Punta Cormorant (Floreana).
VOICE: Call is distinctive, a bat- or mouse-like *jeet* or *eeet.*

BAIRD'S SANDPIPER *Calidris bairdii*   **Plate p. 50**

Sp: Playero de Baird
STATUS: Vagrant.
IDENTIFICATION: Length 19 cm. Another smallish wader with long wings and short legs and bill. Best told apart from White-rumped by slimmer and even more elongated appearance, finer, more pointed bill, and generally browner plumage. Head, upperparts and breast band brownish-grey, contrasting with white underparts. Pale supercilium contrasts with dark crown, cheeks and lores. Legs dark, bill slightly downcurved. In flight rump is dark, with paler sides.
DISTRIBUTION: Has been reported during the northern hemisphere winter months from Española and Santa Fé. Two birds have been found dead at James Bay (Santiago).
VOICE: Usual calls are a low and trilling *preeet,* but sometimes a much harsher *krrt.*

WESTERN

SEMIPALMATED

BAIRD'S

WHITE-RUMPED

PECTORAL SANDPIPER *Calidris melanotos*   **Plate p. 47**

Sp: Tin-Güín

STATUS: Vagrant.

IDENTIFICATION: Length 22 cm. A medium-sized wader with a downcurved bill. Upperparts dark brown, with black feather centres and pale edges, giving 'scalloped' appearance. Crown dark. Face, neck and upper chest buff, streaked with dark brown, ending in a clear-cut band across chest. Rest of underparts white. Legs greenish, bill dark and downcurved.

DISTRIBUTION: Has been reported twice from the Miconia zone (highlands) of Santa Cruz during the northern hemisphere winter months.

VOICE: Flight call is a loud and harsh rattling *chuuk* or *trrit.*

STILT SANDPIPER *Micropalama himantopus*   **Plate p. 49**

Sp: Correlinos Tarsilargo

STATUS: Vagrant.

IDENTIFICATION: Length 22 cm. Elegant, medium-sized wader with long legs and thin, pointed bill. In winter plumage has dark brown mottled upperparts, darker on wing feathers. Head, neck and underparts paler and relatively unmarked, though shows faint dusky shading on breast. Bill long, thin and very slightly downcurved to a sharp point; legs long and yellow-green in colour. In flight shows distinctive white rump.

DISTRIBUTION: Reported during the northern hemisphere winter months on Isabela and Santa Cruz.

VOICE: A series of soft, rattling trills.

WILSON'S PHALAROPE *Phalaropus tricolor*   **Plate p. 51**

Sp: Falaropo de Wilson

STATUS: Migrant.

IDENTIFICATION: Length 24 cm. Larger than Red-necked Phalarope, with very long, straight bill. In non-breeding plumage dark grey upperparts contrast with pale underparts. Dark crown and stripe through eye.

DISTRIBUTION: Reported from brackish-water lagoons on Isabela, Floreana, Santiago, Santa Cruz and Genovesa.

VOICE: Normally silent.

RED-NECKED (NORTHERN) PHALAROPE *Phalaropus lobatus*
Plate p. 51

Sp: Falaropo Norteño

STATUS: Migrant.

IDENTIFICATION: Length 20 cm. Small wader, best identified by its distinctive feeding behaviour, during which it spins rapidly on the surface of the water to disturb morsels of food. In winter, white underparts contrast with streaked grey upperparts. Dark smudge through and behind eye, white forehead and crown. Thin, needle-like bill. In flight, white wing-bar is diagnostic.

DISTRIBUTION: Common migrant to the Galápagos, where it is easily seen during August to April. Can be found resting and feeding on the sea or on saltwater lagoons. Rarely seen on land.

VOICE: A single *klip* is given in flight.

RED (GREY) PHALAROPE *Phalaropus fulicarius*   **Plate p. 51**

Sp: Falaropo Rojo

STATUS: Migrant.

IDENTIFICATION: Length 22 cm. Similar in size, shape and behaviour to other phalaropes, but has shorter, stouter bill. In winter plumage has mainly unstreaked, grey upperparts, and pale underparts. Black face-patch and nape contrasts with white crown.

DISTRIBUTION: Rarely seen in the islands; may be overlooked. Only recorded during the northern hemisphere winter from the waters around Fernandina, San Cristóbal and Punta Cormorant (Floreana).
VOICE: Contact and flight call is a shrill *wit*.

Family Haematopodidae

AMERICAN OYSTERCATCHER *Haematopus palliatus galapagensis*
Plate p. 48

Sp: Ostrero
STATUS: Resident (endemic subspecies).
IDENTIFICATION: Length 47 cm. Distinctive, chunky, black-and-white wader with large, straight orange-red bill. Head, neck and chest black; back and wings brownish-black; rump and wing-bars white; tail black. Rest of underparts white. Bill orange-red, legs pink and quite short for bird of this size. Eye yellow, with red orbital ring. The bill is compressed laterally, for use in opening bivalves. Oystercatchers are usually found in pairs, though groups of adults with young can also be seen.
DISTRIBUTION: Found along the shore on both rocky and sandy beaches, intertidal pools, and sometimes saltwater lagoons.
BREEDING: The courtship involves air and land displays. In the air, the bird performs an erratic flight with exaggerated wingbeats. On land, both members of the pair bow to each other while calling. This eventually leads to mating and nest-building. The nest is a slight depression on the ground, usually amongst sand or pebbles, and a long way from the high-tide line. Lays two or three eggs. Once hatched, the chicks are ready to follow their parents. In case of danger, the chicks will flatten their bodies to the ground and remain still until the threat has passed.
FOOD: Feeds on shrimps, crabs and molluscs.
VOICE: A loud *cleep*.

American Oystercatcher's nest

Family Recurvirostridae

BLACK-NECKED STILT *Himantopus (himantopus) mexicanus*
Plate p. 48

Sp: Tero Real
STATUS: Resident.
IDENTIFICATION: Length 36 cm. Unmistakable. Elegant, unbelievably long-legged wader, with distinctive pied plumage. Upperparts black, except for white rump and tail. Underparts white. Variable black mark around the eye, apart from white eyebrow. Bill black, slender and pointed. Legs very long and pink or red in colour, protruding well beyond the tail in flight. Stilts feed in deep water, and are able to swim if necessary. Both sexes look alike, but on closer examination the female's mantle is brownish.
DISTRIBUTION: Found throughout the islands in all salt and freshwater habitats, inland or on the coast.
BREEDING: Occurs from December to June. The courtship is a complicated and spectacular affair, with an acrobatic air dance being performed by both sexes. The bowl-shaped nest is built with sticks and grass, and has even been found in rock crevices. Generally lays four eggs which are incubated by both parents for about 21 days. The chicks are precocial, being able to run out of the nest and hide within an hour of hatching if necessary.
FOOD: Feeds on crabs, snails, insects, shrimps, other invertebrates and tiny fish present in the lagoons. Although the majority of the diet is animal, some seeds of aquatic plants are also included.
VOICE: Variety of high-pitched piping calls, including *kik-kik-kik-kik*, *kek* and *kee-ack*.

Family Charadriidae

AMERICAN GOLDEN PLOVER *Pluvialis dominica*   **Plate p. 52**

Sp: Playero Dorado
STATUS: Vagrant.
IDENTIFICATION: Length 27 cm. Medium-sized plover. In summer plumage has gold and black upperparts and jet-black underparts, separated by white line running from forehead to chest. In winter plumage much less distinctive, with golden and brown upperparts and paler underparts.
DISTRIBUTION: Reported from Tortuga Bay (Santa Cruz).
VOICE: Calls are given as loud single or double-notes, including a quick *treee* or *cher-wit*.

BLACK-BELLIED (GREY) PLOVER *Pluvialis squatarola*   **Plate p. 52**

Sp: Playero Cabezón
STATUS: Migrant.
IDENTIFICATION: Length 29 cm. In breeding plumage, jet-black underparts contrast with silver and grey upperparts, separated by white stripe. In flight shows white rump and black axillaries below wing. In winter plumage upperparts grey spotted with white, underparts pale grey. Bill and legs black.
DISTRIBUTION: Seen on Fernandina, Floreana and Marchena during most months of the year, suggesting that some individuals spend the summer in the archipelago.
VOICE: A distinctive, loud and melancholy *tee-oo-ee*, falling away in pitch.

SEMIPALMATED PLOVER *Charadrius semipalmatus*   **Plate p. 52**

Sp: Chorlitejo
STATUS: Migrant.
IDENTIFICATION: Length 18 cm. Small, plump wader. Crown and upperparts dark brown, contrasting with snowy-white forehead, throat and underparts, black face-mask and breast band (brown in winter). Legs yellowish-orange; bill short and dark, sometimes showing orange at base.
DISTRIBUTION: Generally found near the shore, or around the edges of lagoons. In the highlands can even be found feeding on grassy areas near freshwater pools. Found all year round, though commoner from August to May. All birds seen in the Galápagos are wintering or non-breeders.
VOICE: Flight call is a sharp whistling *chee-wee* or *chuwit*, rising towards the end.

WILSON'S PLOVER *Charadrius wilsonia*   **Plate p. 52**

Sp: Chorlo de Wilson
STATUS: Vagrant.
IDENTIFICATION: Length 20 cm. Slightly larger than Semipalmated Plover, with a heavier black bill. Crown and upperparts mid-brown, contrasting with white forehead, throat and underparts. Black breast band broader than Semipalmated. Legs pink.
DISTRIBUTION: Three birds were seen at Punta Cormorant (Floreana) in May 1969.
VOICE: A rather high-pitched and quiet *whit* flight call.

KILLDEER *Charadrius vociferus*   **Plate p. 52**

Sp: Playero Gritón
STATUS: Vagrant.
IDENTIFICATION: Length 27 cm. Medium-sized, long-bodied plover, superficially similar to Semipalmated, but much larger, and with two black breast bands. Upperparts dark brown, contrasting with white underparts. Legs yellowish-green.

DISTRIBUTION: Single bird photographed at Punta Tortuga (Isabela) in February 1971.
VOICE: Call is loud and clear, rapid and often repeated. The *kill-dee* call gives the bird its name.

Family Laridae: Subfamily Larinae

SOUTHERN BLACK-BACKED (KELP) GULL *Larus dominicanus*
Plate p. 39
Sp: Gaviota Dominicana
STATUS: Vagrant.
IDENTIFICATION: Length 58 cm, wingspan 128–142 cm. In breeding plumage has white head and rump, rest of upperparts are black. Upperwings black, with white panels towards wingtip, and white trailing edge; underwings greyish-white, except for white 'mirrors' on outer, black primaries. Immatures much browner, with blackish primaries and secondaries.
DISTRIBUTION: A single record of an individual that stayed in the archipelago for two years.

LAVA GULL *Larus fuliginosus*   Plate p. 53
Sp: Gaviota de Lava
STATUS: Endemic.
IDENTIFICATION: Length 53 cm. Distinctive all-dark gull. Adults mainly ash-grey, though darker on wings and paler on belly and vent. Dark hood, white patch around eye. Bill large, heavy and reddish-black; legs black. In flight shows ash-grey wings with darker primaries, contrasting with narrow pale rump and grey tail with dark central feathers. Immatures much browner overall, with pale lower belly.
DISTRIBUTION: Can be seen in bays and on beaches of Santa Cruz, San Cristóbal and Isabela. Roosts on the shores of saltwater lagoons.
BREEDING: A solitary nester, breeding all year round. Nothing is known about the early stages of courtship. Nests have been found beside saline lagoons or small ponds, and along the coastline. They were located far apart from each other, and contained two eggs. The incubation period is around 33 days, and the young fledge at about 60 days. Once the youngsters leave the nest it is thought that they rely on the adult birds for food for two to two-and-a-half weeks.
FOOD: Feeds on fish waste, dead fish, marine invertebrates, placentae of sea lions, newly-hatched marine iguanas and sand worms.

LAUGHING GULL *Larus atricilla* **Plate p. 53**
Sp: Gaviota Reidora
Status: Rare migrant.
Identification: Length 42 cm, wingspan 102 cm. Small to medium-sized gull, with white underparts, dark grey upperparts and black tips to wings. In summer plumage has a dark black head with a red suborbital ring. Legs and bill dark red. In winter plumage the head is white apart from a dark smudge around the eye and crown. In flight shows white rump and tail. Immatures have variable brown mottling on wing feathers, greyish underparts and a black tail band.
Distribution: An uncommon northern hemisphere winter visitor, reported from Isabela, San Cristóbal and Santa Cruz.

FRANKLIN'S GULL *Larus pipixcan* **Plate p. 53**
Sp: Gaviota de Franklin
Status: Migrant.
Identifcation: Length 37 cm, wingspan 91 cm. Superficially similar to Laughing Gull, but smaller and more delicate in build. In summer plumage has dark grey upperparts and black primary feathers with white 'spots' and white tips. Underparts, neck and chest white, head black. In winter plumage has dark patch across and behind eye, extending around back of nape; crown and forehead white. In flight shows black primaries bordered by white crescent and white tip. Bill and legs red in summer, dark in winter. First-winter has paler upperparts with mottled grey-brown on wings, and dark tail band.
Distribution: Common northern hemisphere winter visitor, reported from October to March from San Cristóbal, Isabela, Floreana, Santa Cruz, Baltra and Fernandina.

SWALLOW-TAILED GULL *Larus furcatus* **Plate p. 53**
Sp: Gaviota de Cola Bifurcada
Status: Endemic.
Identification: Length 58 cm, wingspan 130 cm. Highly distinctive, tern-like gull, uniquely adapted to a nocturnal lifestyle. At rest shows grey neck and upperparts, white underparts, black primaries and a dark grey head. At close range the enlarged eye is obvious. Bill dark, tipped with yellow and with a white base. Legs flesh-pink. In flight, has long, pointed wings with distinctive pattern of grey saddle and wing-coverts, white secondaries and black outer primaries. Tail white and deeply forked. Males are larger than females. In non-breeding plumage, has white head with dark eye patch. Immatures have white head, dark eye patch and ear-spot, scaly brown-and-white upperparts, and black tail band. Although several characteristics of this species are tern-like (long, pointed wings and short tail), it has webbed feet like the gulls. The physical adaptations to a nocturnal life include the white colour of the young (unique amongst gulls), which makes them conspicuous at night, the pale tip and base of the bill, and the large eyes.
Distribution: Breeds on all the islands except for Fernadina and the west coast of Isabela.

Breeding: Breeds throughout the year, at cycles of nine or ten months. Males choose the nesting area to which they show great loyalty. Courtship begins with a greeting ceremony, and the nests are placed on rocky cliffs and shores. The nest is made up of a selection of up to 300 small pebbles. The nest has a depression in the centre, in which the female lays a single, spotted egg. The egg is incubated by both parents for about 34 days, and both also take care of the young until they are about 90 days old. The fledglings can be seen swimming in groups near the nesting area. After this period of dependency both parents and offspring leave for four to five months, when they return to start another breeding season.

Food: Feeds at night on fish and squid that come to the surface. Feeding takes place ten to 20 miles (16–32 km) from the nearest land.

Voice: Several different calls, which according to sonograms have characteristics of those used for echolocation. The commonest, an alarm call, is a rattling sound mixed with a piercing *pee*.

Swallow-tailed Gull is the world's only nocturnal gull

Subfamily Sternidae

BLACK TERN *Chlidonias niger*   **Plate p. 39**

Sp: Gaviota Negra

Status: Vagrant.

Identification: Length 22–24 cm, wingspan 66 cm. In breeding plumage has blackish head and slate-grey upperparts, with white vent and undertail-coverts. Upperwings slate-grey, primaries and secondaries dark-tipped. Tail is brownish-grey. In non-breeding plumage, head much whiter, black on crown extends to base of bill through eye; upperparts a much lighter grey. Immatures are browner overall, with mostly whitish underparts and grey tail.

Distribution: The only record is of a single dead immature.

ROYAL TERN *Sterna maxima*   **Plate p. 54**

Sp: Gaviotín Real
STATUS: Migrant.
IDENTIFICATION: Length 51 cm, wingspan 104 cm. Large, gull-sized tern with distinctive, large orange bill. Upperparts pale grey, underparts white. Legs black, bill orange. Black cap in breeding plumage; for rest of year has white on crown and black feathers on rear of crest. Forked tail. In flight appears heavy, almost gull-like in appearance
DISTRIBUTION: Has been reported from June to March on sandy beaches on Santa Cruz and by the Quinta Playa lagoon, southern Isabela.

COMMON TERN *Sterna hirundo*   **Plate p. 54**

Sp: Gaviotín Común
STATUS: Migrant.
IDENTIFICATION: Length 37 cm, wingspan 76 cm. Medium-sized tern, with grey upperparts and white underparts, face and rump. Cap black. Tail long, white, and forked. Legs red; bill orange-red with black tip.
DISTRIBUTION: Has been reported from Santa Cruz, San Cristóbal, Isabela and Española, during the northern hemisphere winter months.

SOOTY TERN *Sterna fuscata*   **Plate p. 54**

Sp: Gaviotín Negro
STATUS: Resident.
IDENTIFICATION: Length 41 cm, wingspan 81 cm. Mainly dark tern, with brownish-black upperparts contrasting strongly with white underparts and forehead. Tail is brown, edged with white, and deeply forked. Legs and bill black. Immature lacks the white of adult, being mainly brown apart from pale linings on underwing.
DISTRIBUTION: Found on Darwin and Wolf, where it breeds in large numbers.

WHITE TERN *Gygis alba*   **Plate p. 39**

Sp: Gaviotín Blanco
STATUS: Vagrant.
IDENTIFICATION: Length 30 cm, wingspan 76 cm. Unmistakable; the only wholly white tern. Small, elegant and with a buoyant flight. Dark legs and bill.
DISTRIBUTION: Reported from Genovesa and also at sea, 300 miles (480 km) southwest of the islands.

COMMON NODDY *Anous stolidus galapagensis*   **Plate p. 54**

Sp: Gaviotín Cabeza Blanca
STATUS: Resident (endemic subspecies).
IDENTIFICATION: Length 39 cm, wingspan 81 cm. Only all-dark tern found in the islands. Apart from pale grey forehead and cap, whole body sooty-brown in

colour, with black legs and bill. Tail not forked, but wedge-shaped, with a small notch at the tip.

DISTRIBUTION: Can be found along the coasts of all the islands.

BREEDING: Breeds throughout the year, mainly between November and July. The courtship involves a complicated series of nodding and bowing movements. Nests are built on rocks that project from the walls of caves formed on the faces of cliffs, barely above the high-tide line. Lays a single egg.

FOOD: Feeds by hovering above the water's surface in large groups, sometimes in the company of shearwaters and storm-petrels. It is commonly seen hovering over swimming pelicans as they fish. Does not plunge-dive. Feeds on small fish.

VOICE: Generally silent, though sometimes utters a low growling sound.

Common Noddy often use a fishing pelican as a source of food and convenient perch

Subfamily Stercorariinae

SOUTH POLAR SKUA *Catharacta maccormicki*   **Plate p. 53**

Sp: Salteador Polar

STATUS: Vagrant.

IDENTIFICATION: Length 53 cm, wingspan 132 cm. Large, bulky skua, superficially resembling a huge immature gull. Plumage generally dark brown, apart from noticeable white flash at base of primaries, and slightly paler across the nape. In flight appears very bulky and broad-winged, though can move surprisingly quickly. It parasitises other seabirds.

DISTRIBUTION: A single sighting off Cabo Berkeley (Isabela).

POMARINE SKUA (JAEGER) *Stercorarius pomarinus*   **Plate p. 53**

Sp: Salteador
Status: Vagrant.
Identification: Length 53 cm, wingspan 122 cm. Powerfully-built seabird, superficially resembling a juvenile gull in appearance. Comes in two distinct plumages: light-phase and dark-phase. Light-phase adult has dark brown upperparts, wings and tail, contrasting with pale underparts and nape, with a dark cap and breast band. Dark-phase appears all dark brown. Wings have pale flashes at bases of primaries in both phases. Immature varies in plumage, though generally more barred than adult. Tail wedge-shaped, with two protruding central feathers (absent in immature). Parasitical on other seabirds, chasing them until they regurgitate or drop their food.
Distribution: Has been sighted in Elizabeth Bay on the west coast of Isabela, and between Española and Floreana.

Note: There have been possible sightings of two other skuas, Arctic and Long-tailed, but no confirmed records to date.

ORDER COLUMBIFORMES

Family Columbidae

The birds of this group, doves and pigeons, have small heads, short legs, pointed wings and fanned tails. Only one species is present in the Galápagos, where it is endemic.

The overall status of Galápagos Dove is unknown, though numbers have considerably increased on Pinzón Island where a rat eradication campaign took place, suggesting that predation from these rodents may be reducing their population on other islands. Cats may also be responsible for reduced numbers on some islands.

Eared Dove

EARED DOVE *Zenaida auriculata*

Sp: Paloma Sabanera
STATUS: Vagrant.
IDENTIFICATION: Length 23 cm. Upperparts in male olive-brown; flanks and underwing-coverts bluish-grey; belly and throat pinkish-cinnamon; head grey, with two distinct black marks on sides. Female more greyish-brown overall. Tail pointed, all but central feathers white- or cinnamon-tipped.
DISTRIBUTION: A single record.

GALÁPAGOS DOVE *Zenaida galapagoensis*   **Plate p. 55**

Sp: Paloma de Galápagos
STATUS: Endemic.
IDENTIFICATION: Length 20 cm. Upperparts reddish-brown with black spots and some white on the wingtips. Underparts mostly pinkish-brown. Neck has an iridescent bronze-green shine. Legs and feet red. Bright blue ring around the eyes. A cream stripe fringed with black runs from the bottom of the eye to the lower neck. Bill more curved than that of other doves. Male and female alike, immature duller. Populations on Darwin and Wolf Islands are considered to be a separate subspecies based on their considerably larger size.
DISTRIBUTION: Present on Darwin, Wolf, Santa Cruz, San Cristóbal, Floreana, Santiago, Pinzón, Pinta, Marchena, Genovesa, Española, Santa Fé, and Fernandina. Prefers the drier lowlands, where it may be found singly or in small groups.
BREEDING: Reproduces from February to June, about three weeks after the first rains. The courtship involves an aerial display and a bowing ceremony on land, accompanied by the male's deep cooing call. The nest is built on the bare ground, beneath plate-like pieces of lava, or on *Opuntia* plants. The species also sometimes uses old mockingbird nests. Generally lays two eggs, with an incubation period of about 14 days. The fledging period is also about 14 days.
FOOD: Feeding varies with the availability of different foods throughout the seasons. From the first rains to the end of the laying period feeds mainly on caterpillars. On Genovesa and Wolf, where *Opuntia* does not have sharp spines, it also feeds on the cactus flowers and pollen. During the hatching and fledging periods feeds on the seeds of *Croton scouleri*. By the time all the young have fledged, fruits and seeds of other plants are ready and are also eaten by the doves. During the remainder of the year, it feeds on seeds that have fallen on the ground and, where possible, on *Opuntia* flowers and pulp.
VOICE: The male produces a quiet, cooing sound.

ORDER CUCULIFORMES

Family Cuculidae
Cuckoos have slender bodies, rounded wings, a curved upper mandible and long tails whose outer feathers are shorter than the inside ones, making the tail appear rounded.

There are three representatives of this family in the Galápagos: a resident, a rare migrant and an introduced species. The resident Dark-billed Cuckoo is present in low numbers and its status is unknown. The introduced Smooth-billed Ani has caused much debate, being the focus of an eradication campaign which was never completed. Their population now seems to be increasing. Their effect on the native species is unknown.

BLACK-BILLED CUCKOO *Coccyzus erythropthalmus*   **Plate p. 55**

Sp: Cuclillo Pico Negro
STATUS: Vagrant (one record).
IDENTIFICATION: Length 31 cm. Brown upperparts, with slightly warmer tone on primaries. Underparts white. Bill black. Adult has red orbital ring. Tail grey with pale tips.
DISTRIBUTION: Only one record, in 1970, when an immature was found dead on Española. The species is common in eastern North America.

DARK-BILLED CUCKOO *Coccyzus melacoryphus*   **Plate p. 55**

Sp: Cuclillo
STATUS: Resident.
IDENTIFICATION: Length 28 cm. Slender, with very long tail. Upperparts generally dull greyish-brown, more rufous on wings. Nape and crown grey, black ear-coverts. Underparts rusty yellow. Legs and bill black. Long tail feathers brown with white tips. Very shy, so normally only seen in flight. Often heard rather than seen.
DISTRIBUTION: Found on Isabela, Fernandina, Santa Cruz, San Cristóbal, Floreana, Santiago and Pinzón.
BREEDING: Habits on Galápagos not known.
FOOD: Feeds mainly on insects.
VOICE: Produces a low chuckling call.

SMOOTH-BILLED ANI *Crotophaga ani*   **Plate p. 55**

Sp: Garrapatero Común
STATUS: Introduced.
IDENTIFICATION: Length 30–36 cm. Uniformly black bird, with short wings, very long tail, and a heavy, smooth black bill. It is the only large black landbird on the islands.
DISTRIBUTION: Found in the farm zones (highlands) of Isabela, Santa Cruz, and Floreana. There is a group of a dozen or so birds on Santiago. Has been eradicated from Santa Fé and Pinzón. In wet years it can also establish itself in the lowlands. Usually seen during the day in groups of ten to 40 birds in areas near cattle, with which the species frequently associates. Records of Groove-billed Ani are most likely to have been Smooth-billed.
BREEDING: Reproduces during the rainy season (December to May). Builds its cup-shaped nest in low branches of thickets where it is very difficult to find.

Incubation and fledging periods are of about 14 days each.

Feeding: Feeds on insects, mainly grasshoppers and crickets. Also feeds on larvae of dipterans (two-winged insects) and on other insects and spiders present in grassy areas.

Voice: Many different calls. The most common is the alarm: an unmistakable two-note call *aa-ak, aa-ak, aa-ak*, repeated several times.

ORDER STRIGIFORMES

Owls are amongst the most characteristic of all birds, with short necks, large eyes and a characteristic heart-shaped face. They are mostly nocturnal, flying on silent wings in search of their prey.

Two species of owl are resident in the Galápagos, Barn and Short-eared, both with endemic subspecies. Their status is uncertain, though following the 1982 census the population for each species has been estimated to be around the 9,000 mark. On San Cristóbal and Isabela, owls are hunted by the inhabitants because they prey on chickens, but the effect of this hunting on the owl populations has not been determined. It is possible that they are also hunted in the other populated islands. Both species of owls in the Galápagos have smaller clutch sizes and slower development of young than their mainland counterparts.

Family Tytonidae

BARN OWL *Tyto alba punctatissima*   Plate p. 46

Sp: Lechuza Blanca (de Campanario)

Status: Resident (endemic subspecies).

Identification: Length 26 cm, wingspan 68 cm. Upperparts golden brown, delicately speckled with light and dark; underparts almost white. The heart-shaped face is characteristic. Has relatively long legs and small eyes. Smaller in size and darker in colour than the continental forms. Male and female alike.

Distribution: Found on Fernandina, Isabela, Santiago, Santa Cruz and San Cristóbal. Prefers the dry and poorly vegetated lowlands, although can be found in the highlands as well.

Breeding: In the highlands breeds during the months of November to May. In the lowlands nests have been found with eggs in every month of the year. The nests are placed in small cavities in the ground, in walls of lava tubes or in volcanic cones. Occasionally nests are found in holes in the trunks or between the roots of *Psidium* trees. Lays an average of three eggs which are incubated for about 30 days. The youngsters fledge at about 75 days.

Food: The Barn Owl is nocturnal, leaving its roosting place in tree holes, cavities or abandoned buildings between the hours of 18.30 and 19.00, and returning from its hunting activities at about 05.30 the next morning. It hunts from a perch or 'on foot' and its main prey are small rats, mice and insects, although

it does occasionally feed on landbirds. The average size of its prey is 35 grams, on average 60 per cent smaller than that taken on the mainland.
Voice: Produces a cat-like cry which is rarely heard.

Family Strigidae

SHORT-EARED OWL *Asio flammeus galapagoensis*   **Plate p. 46**
Sp: Lechuza de Campo
Status: Resident (endemic subspecies).
Identification: Length 34–42 cm; wingspan 90–105 cm. Fairly large, mainly brown-looking owl, usually seen in flight. Upperparts blotched cream, light and dark brown; underparts paler, also blotched and streaked with brown. Eyes large and yellow. The ear-tufts that give the species its name are often hard to see, but may sometimes be prominent. In flight, looks almost harrier-like, owing to long, fairly pointed wings and habit of quartering low over the ground in search of prey. Female much larger than male.
Distribution: Found on all the islands except for Fernandina, Wolf and Darwin. Prefers the moist highlands, although can sometimes be found on the coast near seabird colonies. Roosts under bushes, and in outcrops, crevices and banana groves. Since its habits are more diurnal this species is generally easier to observe than Barn Owl.
Breeding: Reproduces during the months of November to May. The nests are placed mainly on the bare ground although they have been also found between roots of trees. Lays three to four eggs. The exact length of the incubation and fledging periods are not known, but after 54 days the young owls are still dependent on their parents. The normal number of chicks fledged is two.
Food: Active mostly during the early morning and late evening, between 05.00 and 10.00, and from 16.00 to 22.00. However, where Galápagos Hawk is also present, the owl becomes nocturnal. As with Barn Owl, Short-eared Owl also hunts from a perch. The main food is small birds and mice, but the species has been known to prey on much larger birds, such as Dark-rumped Petrel chicks and even fledglings.
Voice: During the breeding season produces a barking sound, otherwise is generally silent.

ORDER CAPRIMULGIFORMES

Family Caprimulgidae
Nightjars are mainly nocturnal, falcon-like birds with a characteristic bark-like plumage of greys and browns. They have small bills, large mouths, large heads, short legs and sometimes show white patches on their wings and/or tails.

COMMON NIGHTHAWK *Chordeiles minor*   **Plate p. 55**
Sp: Aguaitacamino Migratorio
STATUS: Migrant.
IDENTIFICATION: Length 24 cm; wingspan 38 cm. A slender, mainly brownish-grey bird with long, crooked wings and a long tail. Upperparts dark grey, mottled with brown, with dark unmarked flight feathers. Underparts barred grey and brown. Small white band across throat. In flight, appears all dark with conspicuous white oval patches across primaries. Legs so short that the bird has to perch sideways on branches.
DISTRIBUTION: Has been reported from Española, Isabela, Fernandina and Santa Cruz. Could be confused with another American species, Lesser Nighthawk, though this close relative has slightly shorter and blunter wings.

ORDER APODIFORMES

Family Apodidae
Swifts are fast-flying birds, spending most of their life on the wing, preying on airborne insects. They are characterised by long, scimitar-shaped wings and cylindrical bodies, perfectly adapted for life in the air.

Chimney Swift

CHIMNEY SWIFT *Chaetura pelagica*

Sp: Vencejo de Chimenea
STATUS: Vagrant.
IDENTIFICATION: Length 13 cm. A small, blackish-grey swift, with cigar-shaped body and short, square-ended tail. Has loud chattering call.
DISTRIBUTION: One record.

ORDER CORACIIFORMES

Family Alcedinidae

Kingfishers are characteristically bright-coloured birds, with large heads, and long, sharp bills used to catch fish and other prey. Some species hover in mid-air.

BELTED KINGFISHER *Ceryle alcyon*　　　　　**Plate p. 55**

Sp: Martín Pescador Migratorio
STATUS: Migrant.
IDENTIFICATION: Length 33 cm. Large kingfisher, with prominent blue crest and mainly blue-and-white plumage. Upperparts, wings and head greyish-blue; throat, neck and underparts white with a broad greyish-blue ring across the chest. Female has a rusty ring on belly. Undertail feathers barred with white.
DISTRIBUTION: Has been reported from Santa Cruz, Daphne, Genovesa, Española, Isabela and Floreana. All observations between October and March. This is the most common kingfisher in North America.

ORDER PASSERIFORMES

Family Tyrannidae

VERMILLION FLYCATCHER *Pyrocephalus rubinus*　　　**Plate p. 56**

Sp: Pajaro Brujo
STATUS: Resident.
IDENTIFICATION: Length 14 cm. Unmistakable. The only small, bright red-and-black bird likely to be seen on the islands. Adult male has bright red crown, throat and underparts, and black neck, undertail, wings and upperparts. Also has black mask across eyes. Immature male is pink instead of red. Female has brown upperparts, undertail and underwings, and yellow underparts, with the hint of a brown mask. The male is territorial, performing a distinctive display: flying up in steps peeping and clapping its mandible at each step; then suddenly plunging towards the earth, rising up again before reaching ground. It repeats this display several times.

DISTRIBUTION: Nests on Santa Cruz, San Cristóbal, Isabela, Fernandina, Pinta, Marchena, Santiago, Pinzón and Floreana. Has been reported occasionally on Santa Fé, Rábida, Wolf and Española. Never recorded on Darwin, Baltra or Genovesa.

BREEDING: Not much is known about the breeding behaviour. Breeds during the months of December to May, although possibly also reproduces in the highlands during the remainder of the year if water is abundant. Builds a cup-shaped nest. Female incubates.

FOOD: Feeds mainly on insects that are caught in flight.

VOICE: Has a melodious song which consists of a quick, high sputtering.

GALÁPAGOS FLYCATCHER *Myiarchus magnirostris*   Plate p. 56

Sp: Papamoscas

STATUS: Endemic.

IDENTIFICATION: Length 16 cm. Male and female alike. A little larger than Vermillion Flycatcher, with head and upperparts brownish grey, neck and throat pale grey. Remainder of breast and belly pale yellow, though not as bright as female Vermillion. Faint double wing-bar on closed wing. Large black bill.

DISTRIBUTION: Present on all the islands except for Genovesa, Darwin and Wolf. Prefers the lowlands, although can also be found in the highlands. Extremely friendly, often approaching observers, following them on their walks, and even accepting flies from the hand.

BREEDING: Nests during the wet season from December to May. The nest is placed wherever there is a hole (trees, cactus stumps, etc.).

FOOD: Feeds on flying insects and caterpillars.

VOICE: Melodious song, with a fluid *wheet-we* or *wheet-wheet-we* call (Harris 1974).

EASTERN KINGBIRD *Tyrannus tyrannus*   Plate p. 56

Sp: Pitirre Americano

STATUS: Vagrant.

IDENTIFICATION: Length 22 cm. Adult has black head, slate-grey back and broad white terminal tail band. Underparts white, with pale grey wash to breast. Immature has browner upperparts and darker breast. Favours a wide range of habitats in breeding areas. Calls are a mixture of harsh and more muted twitterings.

DISTRIBUTION: Sighted in 1983, on Genovesa, during the biggest El Niño event in recorded history.

Family Vireonidae

RED-EYED VIREO *Vireo olivaceus*   **Plate p. 57**
Sp: Julián Chiuí Ojirajo
STATUS: Vagrant.
IDENTIFICATION: Length 15 cm. A large, stocky vireo, resembling a thick-billed wood-warbler. Upperparts dark olive-brown, with darker wings and tail. Underparts whitish. Crown pale grey, with white supercilium bordered above and below with black. At close range red eye visible.
DISTRIBUTION: Has been reported from Wolf, during the 1982–83 El Niño event.

Family Mimidae
Mockingbirds are brown or grey and have long tails, short wings and thin bills. Their songs are loud and repetitive, containing many 'borrowed' sounds from which the birds get their name.

There are four species of mockingbirds present in the Galápagos, all endemic. One species is fairly widespread, while the other three are confined to single islands and their satellites. One species, Charles Mockingbird, is listed as rare in the ICBP-IUCN *Red Data Book*.

Mockingbirds in Galápagos are inquisitive and noisy. The only species that has been studied in some detail is Galápagos Mockingbird, though the other three species are thought to show similar behaviour. In general, the Galápagos and Chatham Mockingbirds are smaller, have shorter bills, show more grey on the upperparts and have whiter underparts than Hood and Charles Mockingbirds. The colour of the eyes and the song are species specific.

GALÁPAGOS MOCKINGBIRD *Nesomimus parvulus*   **Plate p. 58**
Sp: Cucuve de Galápagos
STATUS: Endemic.
IDENTIFICATION: Length 25 cm. Streaked, thrush-like bird, with curved beak and long, fan-shaped tail. Darkish grey upperparts, browner on the wings (which have white tips), and a white band across the back of the neck. Underparts and undertail-coverts white, with some streaking on sides of breast. Tail dark. Eye yellowish-green, with a grey-brown patch over the eye.
DISTRIBUTION: Found on Santa Cruz, Santiago, Santa Fé, Isabela, Fernandina, Pinta, Marchena, Genovesa, Darwin and Wolf.
BREEDING: Activities start about a week after the first rains. Nests in trees and lays three or four eggs. Incubation lasts about 15 days. Young fledge after another 17 days, but remain dependent for up to five weeks after leaving the nest, by which time their parents are usually engaged with a second clutch. Galápagos Mockingbird has a special social organisation where older offspring help to feed their younger siblings and defend their parents' territory. During the non-breeding season these family groups stay together.
FOOD: Omnivorous, eating everything from seeds and insects to sea lions'

placentae and other birds' eggs and chicks, notably those of Red-footed Booby, Great Frigatebird, Lava Gulls and Wedge-rumped Storm Petrel. On Santa Fé the mockingbird has a symbiotic relationship with iguanas, feeding on parasites from the reptiles' skin.

VOICE: Very varied, mimicking the songs of many other species, even including the introduced newcomer, Smooth-billed Ani.

CHARLES MOCKINGBIRD *Nesomimus trifasciatus*   Plate p. 58

Sp: Cucuve de Floreana

STATUS: Endemic, rare.

IDENTIFICATION: Length 25 cm. Also very similar to Galápagos Mockingbird, with dark brownish-grey upperparts, dirty white underparts, with some brown forming a band across the chest. The eyes are red-brown and do not have a dark patch over them.

BREEDING: Very little is known. Only nests on *Opuntia* cacti.

FOOD: Feeds mainly on *Opuntia*, but also has been seen pecking at eggs of Blue-footed Booby.

DISTRIBUTION: Found exclusively on Champion and Gardner, satellite islets of Floreana. This species was once also found on Floreana, but became extinct for unknown reasons, though introduced cats have been mentioned as a possible cause. The population has been estimated at 150 birds.

HOOD MOCKINGBIRD *Nesomimus macdonaldi*   Plate p. 58

Sp: Cucuve de Española

STATUS: Endemic.

IDENTIFICATION: Length 28 cm. The largest of the islands' mockingbirds, with a distinctive heavy bill and long legs, though still very similar in overall appearance to the other species. Upperparts greyish-brown, underparts whitish-grey. The band separating the head from the neck is very faint. Eyes yellowish, with a dark patch over them. During the non-breeding season, gathers in groups of up to 40 individuals feeding in the same area. May be very aggressive and it is reluctant to fly, preferring to move through the vegetation on foot.

FOOD: Feeds on almost anything, having even been reported probing its bill into the sand looking for food. Pecks at eggs of Waved Albatross, Blue-footed and Masked Boobies, Swallow-tailed Gull, American Oystercatcher and Galápagos Dove.

DISTRIBUTION: Found only on Española and its satellite islet Gardner.

CHATHAM MOCKINGBIRD *Nesomimus melanotis*   Plate p. 58

Sp: Cucuve de San Cristóbal

STATUS: Endemic

IDENTIFICATION: Length 25 cm. Very similar to previous species, being intermediate in plumage between Galápagos and Hood Mockingbirds. Upperparts brownish-grey, underparts white, with white band separating the head from the

back. Wing feathers have white tips. Eyes greenish surrounded by a white patch. A brown mark extends from the forehead to the white eye patch and from there to the neck.
Food: Same as other mockingbirds found in the archipelago.
Distribution: Found exclusively on San Cristóbal.

Family Bombycillidae

CEDAR WAXWING *Bombycilla cedrorum*   **Plate p. 57**
Sp: Miracielito
Status: Vagrant.
Identification: Length 18 cm. Male and female alike, and unmistakable. A medium-sized passerine, generally brown in colour, with a prominent crest and black mask. Upperparts and breast uniform brown, shading to yellow on the belly. Wings darker brown, rump grey. Tail short and black with yellow tip and white undertail-coverts.
Distribution: Reported from Genovesa during El Niño of 1982–83.

Family Hirundinidae

PURPLE MARTIN *Progne subis*   **Plate p. 59**
Sp: Golondrina de Iglesias
Status: Migrant.
Identification: Length 19 cm. A large, bulky swallow. Male uniform steel-blue, with a glossy sheen produced by the tips of the feathers, especially on the head, body and upperwings. Female also dark blue, but duller, with grey forehead and greyish underparts. Juvenile has grey-brown head and upperparts, off-white underparts.
Distribution: Females and immatures have been reported from Española and Santa Cruz. As males are easily confused with Galápagos Martin there are no confirmed records.

GALÁPAGOS MARTIN *Progne modesta modesta*   **Plate p. 59**
Sp: Golondrina de Galápagos
Status: Endemic race of Southern Martin (found widely on mainland).
Identification: Length 15 cm. A medium-sized, uniformly-coloured swallow, with long, broad wings and a narrow, slightly-forked tail. Male uniform blue-black apart from sooty-grey underwings, appearing wholly dark in flight. Females sooty-black above, dark brown below. Immatures mainly brown, though males sometimes show traces of blue in their plumage. Smaller than Purple Martin, males of which can be confused with this species. Flies on stiff wings, alternating rapid wingbeats with glides.

DISTRIBUTION: Found on all the islands except Wolf, Darwin, Marchena, Pinta, Rábida and Genovesa. On Española has not been found nesting. Found in a variety of habitats from the highlands to the shore.
BREEDING: Nests between August and March, laying two or three white eggs in holes and crevices.
FOOD: Feeds on insects caught while flying.
VOICE: A variety of calls, including a short warble, a short, harsh contact call, and a high-pitched alarm.

SAND MARTIN (BANK SWALLOW) *Riparia riparia*   Plate p. 59
Sp: Golondrina Parda
STATUS: Migrant.
IDENTIFICATION: Length 12 cm. A small, compact brown-and-white swallow, with a short, square tail. Male and female alike. Upperparts mid-brown, darker on the wings. Underparts white with a brown breast band.
DISTRIBUTION: Individuals found on Española, Genovesa and San Cristóbal.

BARN SWALLOW *Hirundo rustica*   Plate p. 59
Sp: Golondrina de Horquilla
STATUS: Migrant.
IDENTIFICATION: Length 18 cm. The typical swallow: elegant, delicate and low-flying. Male and female alike. Head and upperparts dark blue, with a chestnut forehead and throat, blue chest band and pale underparts.
DISTRIBUTION: Reported from Floreana, Española, San Cristóbal and Santa Cruz during the northern hemisphere winter months.

CLIFF SWALLOW *Petrochelidon pyrrhonota*   Plate p. 59
Sp: Golondrina Risquera
STATUS: Vagrant.
IDENTIFICATION: Length 13 cm. A small, compact swallow, showing a square tail and distinctive pale rump in flight. Male and female alike. Back blue, streaked with white; wings brown; rusty rump, dark tail. Blue cap with white forehead and chestnut face, chin and throat. Underparts dirty greyish-white.
DISTRIBUTION: Only one bird reported, 60 miles north of Darwin.

Family Fringillidae: Subfamily Geospizinae

Following Lack and Grant, I have divided this family into six genera comprising 14 species. However, the systematics of Darwin's Finches are complex and controversial, with much debate amongst scientists about how they should be categorised. The situation is further complicated by the discovery that different populations of a single species can show as many differences from each other as from so-called 'separate species'. Clearly, this fascinating group is in a state of almost visible evolutionary flux, and much further study is needed.

The four groups commonly recognised are as follows: ground-finches, all belonging to the genus *Geospiza*; tree-finches, belonging to the genera *Camarhynchus, Platyspiza* and *Cactospiza;* and two other genera with only a single member each, *Certhidia* and *Pinaroloxias* (on Cocos Island).

BREEDING: All finches share similar reproductive behaviour, with only minor differences between species. After the first rains the otherwise sociable finches start forming territories and defending them from intruders. Males drive away males and females of their own species while females attack females or immature males. The male displays threat postures throughout his territory and sings while perched or flying. Intruders are chased away after an initial threat.

Often finches will permit intruders in their territory if they are feeding, but if they show any kind of reproductive behaviour they will be treated as rivals. Males build several nests and display for the females. Once a female is interested she chooses one of the nests the territorial male has built, or builds a new one with the male. In the lowlands nests are built with grass, twigs and wild cotton. In the highlands lichens are also used. The nest is cup-shaped, with a domed roof and a side entrance. Nests are often lined with white feathers.

Besides nest-building, courtship also involves bill-touching, and chasing of the female by the male. After some chasing she may adopt the copulation posture: motionless with bill pointing towards the sky. The female lays two to five eggs that she incubates alone for about 12 days. She lays one egg every day and starts to incubate before the clutch is completed, during which time she is fed by the male. However, if the weather is hot enough, the female may leave the nest to feed on her own. The female always takes a break to feed at intervals of about 15–30 minutes (variable).

Once hatched the chicks are fed by both parents—on a diet including caterpillars, spiders, pollen, fruit and seeds. The young leave the nest after 13 to 16 days. Normally, the males will learn the species' song from their father, but on occasions they learn the song of another finch species.

Breeding lasts until May, but in abnormally wet years it continues as long as the rains continue. The birds moult their feathers after the breeding season in a process that takes two to three months. But if rains start again, moulting is interrupted and the birds resume breeding.

FOOD: The finches feed on a wide variety of foods, varying their diet seasonally depending on what is available and the ages and shapes of their bills. For example, at the beginning of the rainy season, when the plants start to bud and flower, most finches will use this resource. Later, when insect larvae and fruits are available, the birds will feed on them. During the garúa season they feed on seeds remaining on the ground.

VOICE: Bowman (1983) divided finch songs into three groups.

The **whistle song**, produced during the breeding season is either a long continuous hissing note or a series of short hiss-like notes. Both calls start at high frequencies, ending either abruptly or gradually at lower frequencies.

The **basic song** is used in territorial advertising or defence. There are three variations to this call. The 'basic song proper' has a long, buzzy middle note (*chic-a.a.a.a.a.a.-go*). The 'special basic song' is a long, rasping *bizzzzz*. The 'abbreviate basic song' is a basic song where the middle note has been considerably shortened (*ree-search, ree-search*).

The **derive song** is used in a similar way to the basic song. This song can be polysyllabic (*tee-you, tee-you; chee-tee, chee-tee*) or monosyllabic (*churr-churr-churr-churr-churr*).

He found that the song of the finches was highly variable. Variations occurred both within populations of the same species and within different species. The variation in the calls of different populations of the same species was related to habitat type. Some populations of a species borrowed calls from other species, making the identification of Galápagos finches, by song alone, incredibly difficult. For more detailed information about the vocalisations of Darwin's finches refer to Bowman's paper.

CONSERVATION STATUS IN GALÁPAGOS: With the exception of Floreana Large Ground-finch, *Geospiza magnirostris magnirostris*, and Mangrove Finch, *Camarhynchus heliobates*, which are considered as Indeterminate and Vulnerable respectively in the ICBP-IUCN *Red Data Book*, all the other species of Darwin's Finches survive in large numbers.

GROUND-FINCHES: Genus *Geospiza*

Males black; females and immatures have brown and streaked upperparts and underparts, darker above than below. The shade of brown and the amount of spots on the females varies from species to species.

Immature males pass through a five-stage moulting process until they acquire their final coloration: with black appearing first on the back, then on the throat, chest and belly before finally covering the entire underparts with the exception of the undertail which is typically white. In adults the bill turns from yellow to black during the breeding season.

Although identification of species of ground-finch by song alone is often impossible, some generalities have been found. Smaller-billed species have a faster delivery of songs and a higher modal frequency than larger species. The whistle call is a single *hisssss*, longer in the larger species. While all species sing the basic, derive and whistle songs, the special basic song has only been recorded in some populations of Sharp-beaked Ground-finch.

LARGE GROUND-FINCH *Geospiza magnirostris* **Plate p. 60**

Sp: Pinzón Grande de Tierra
STATUS: Endemic.
WEIGHT: 35 g.
IDENTIFICATION: Has the largest bill-to-head ratio, and strong head and mandible muscles, allowing it to feed on big, hard seeds. Male black; female has brown upperparts and streaked underparts. Specimens collected from the population in Darwin Island show great bill variation and it has been suggested that this occurs as a result of hybridisation between *G. magnirostris* and *G. conirostris*.
DISTRIBUTION: Found on all islands except Seymour, Baltra, San Cristóbal (extinct), Floreana (extinct?), Santa Fé (extinct?) and Española. It is not known if it breeds on Plazas. Prefers the coastal and transitional zones.
FOOD: Feeds on trees or on the ground. Food includes native fruits and berries, nectar of muyuyo (*Cordia lutea*), flowers of *Croton*, green leaves, caterpillars and seeds.
VOICE: Produces the songs at a slower tempo, more melodious and forceful than other ground-finches.

MEDIUM GROUND-FINCH *Geospiza fortis* **Plate p. 60**

Sp: Pinzón Mediano de Tierra
STATUS: Endemic
WEIGHT: 20 g.
IDENTIFICATION: Although the bill-size varies considerably, it is always smaller than that of the Large Ground-finch, but bigger than the bill of the Small Ground-finch. Male black; female has brown upperparts and streaked underparts.
DISTRIBUTION: Found on all islands except Genovesa, Española, Darwin and

Finch picking parasites from the skin of an iguana while mockingbirds (left) look on

126

Wolf. Prefers the lowlands and transitional zones, although can be found feeding in the farm zones. Uncommon in forests.

Food: Feeds on fallen fruits of poison apple, tree flowers, leaf buds, young green leaves, caterpillars, seeds and small insects. Some individuals have been seen cleaning parasites from the skin of giant tortoises on Alcedo volcano, Isabela and marine iguanas on Plazas.

Voice: Has the widest range of songs of the Geospizinae, varying greatly within the same population.

SMALL GROUND-FINCH *Geospiza fuliginosa*   Plate p. 60

Sp: Pinzón Pequeno de Tierra
Status: Endemic.
Weight: 14 g.
Identification: Small Ground-finch, and Sharp-beaked Ground-finch of Genovesa are similar in size. To distinguish between them it is important to consider not only the bill shape but also the distribution. The bill of Small Ground-finch is more conical, and shorter. Male black; female has brown upperparts and streaked underparts.
Distribution: Present on all the islands except for Genovesa, Darwin and Wolf. Prefers the coastal and transitional zones but often feeds in the highlands. It moves to the highlands, some times in large numbers, during the non-breeding season.
Food: Has the most varied diet of all the finches: grass seeds, *Opuntia* flowers, green buds and leaves, flowers, small green caterpillars, small seeds and insects, pulp of fallen *Opuntia*, carrion, introduced fruits, refuse, and marine worms. Small Ground-finch has symbiotic relationships with Galápagos tortoises (on Isabela, Santa Cruz and Pinzón), marine iguanas (Fernandina, Española and Santa Cruz) and land iguanas (Fernandina and Plazas)—feeding on the skin parasites of these reptiles.
Voice: This species uses mainly disyllabic songs, which are delivered more quickly than is the case in other species.

SHARP-BEAKED GROUND-FINCH *Geospiza difficilis*   Plate p. 60

Sp: Pinzón Vampiro (northern populations)
Status: Endemic.
Weight: 20 g.
Identification: (See Small Ground-finch for additional information.) This species shows great variation among the different populations, with three distinct subspecies, raising questions about whether they are in fact separate species. Male black, with rufous, instead of white, undertail-coverts; in some populations female with darker upperparts and more streaked underparts than Small, Medium and Large Ground-finches. Some scientists question whether the population from Genovesa is actually *G. fuliginosa* rather than *G. difficilis*, but so far this problem has not been resolved.
Distribution: Found on Fernandina, Santiago, Pinta, Genovesa, Darwin and

Wolf. It has become extinct on Santa Cruz and Floreana, and is thought to be extinct on Isabela and San Cristóbal. It is normally found in the highlands, except on Genovesa, Darwin and Wolf, where in the absence of high ground the bird occupies the coastal zone. During the non-breeding season, it disperses to the lowlands.

FOOD: Feeds on green leaves, cactus pulp, flowers (pollen and nectar) and anthropods found under debris on the forest floor. The subspecies found on Wolf and Darwin (Vampire Finch) feeds on insects found on the backs of Masked Boobies. It also pecks at the base of the boobies' feathers until they bleed, then feeds on the blood. Sometimes cracks open Sooty Tern eggs.

VOICE: There are significant inter-island differences in song structure, but the general pattern outlined earlier still holds true for this species.

COMMON CACTUS-FINCH *Geospiza scandens*   Plate p. 60

Sp: Pinzón del Cactus

STATUS: Endemic.

WEIGHT: 21 g.

IDENTIFICATION: Male black; female has brownish-grey upperparts and streaked underparts. The bill is longer proportionally than the other ground finches.

DISTRIBUTION: Found on all the islands except Darwin, Wolf, Genovesa, Española and Fernandina. This species became extinct on Pinzón after 1906, but was found again in 1984; it is not known if the birds are breeding there. Restricted to the areas where *Opuntia* is present.

FOOD: Specialised in feeding on *Opuntia* cacti. Has a more pronounced split tongue than the other finches, like that of hummingbirds and other nectar-feeding birds. Feeds upon *Opuntia* flowers, fruits and insects found around the spines. Also feeds on caterpillars, grass seed and introduced fruits. Obtains all its water from *Opuntia* pulp.

VOICE: Similar to Large Cactus-finch, but there are remarkable inter-island differences in the structure of the song.

LARGE CACTUS-FINCH *Geospiza conirostris*   Plate p. 60

Sp: Pinzón Grande de Cactus

STATUS: Endemic.

Weight: 28 g.

IDENTIFICATION: Male black; the female is the darkest female of all the ground-finches, although the standard pattern of brown upperparts and streaked underparts is maintained. The bill is flattened on the sides and the lower mandible is flatter and less convex in profile than that of the other ground-finches. There are three different subspecies. The population on Genovesa resembles the population of *G. scandens* on Marchena to the point at which it may simply be a highly differentiated form of that species. The same applies to the populations from Española, which are very similar to *G. fortis* or *C. magnirostris*.

DISTRIBUTION: Found only on Genovesa, Española and Gardner (see Large Ground-finch for more information).

FOOD: Probes *Opuntia* flowers, eats *Acacia* leaves, *Croton* fruits and also picks seeds and insects off the ground.

VOICE: On Española, the song has extended trills, resembling the calls of Red-winged Blackbirds in North America.

Genus *Platyspiza*

VEGETARIAN FINCH *Platyspiza crassirostris*   Plate p. 61
Sp: Pinzón Vegetariano

STATUS: Endemic.

WEIGHT: 34 g

IDENTIFICATION: Male has black upperparts, head, neck, chest, wings and tail, and a white belly, with some black streaking on flanks. Female resembles ground-finches, with plain olive-brown upperparts, olive rump, and less streaked underparts. Very short, deep and broad bill, with deeply decurved upper mandible.

DISTRIBUTION: Found on Isabela, Fernandina, Santa Cruz, Santiago, Floreana, Marchena, Pinta and Rábida. It is extinct from Pinzón, and possibly from Santa Fé. May be found wherever there are tall trees, but generally only breeds in the transitional and highland zones up to the tree limit.

FOOD: Feeds on blossom, buds and young leaves of trees. On the ground feeds on leaves of herbaceous plants and occasionally caterpillars. Likes to feed on the introduced papaya.

VOICE: Like Large Cactus-finch, this species has a song similar to that of Red-winged Blackbird in North America. It produces several rather musical notes that converge in a *churrr* . Sometimes a descending *hiss* is added to the song, often ending with a distinct whistled note at a slightly lower pitch (Bowman 1983).

TREE-FINCHES: Genus *Camarhynchus*
All the species of this genus show sexual dimorphism in colour: brownish-green males with black heads, and females brownish-green with less striation on the underparts than female ground-finches. The tree-finches have a disyllabic note which is repeated very rapidly in groups of three: *tchur-wee, tchur-wee, tchur-wee*. They may move towards the lowlands in the non-breeding season.

The songs of the three species of *Camarhynchus* are similar in frequency spread, but the distribution of the energy peaks is different, with increased energy in lower frequencies as you move from small to large species. The special basic songs of all three species are so similar that field identification is not possible. The whistled songs are virtually indistinguishable (Bowman 1983), although very different from the whistle of *Cactospiza* and therefore useful in separating the members of one genera from the other. The whistle song of tree-finches comprises several *hiss*-like notes, *see-see-see-see-see-see*, contrasting with the single-note whistle of *Cactospiza*.

LARGE TREE-FINCH *Camarhynchus psittacula*   **Plate p. 61**

Sp: Pinzón Grande de Árbol

STATUS: Endemic.

WEIGHT: 18 g.

IDENTIFICATION: Male has black head and brownish-grey upperparts with an olivaceous tint, and whitish underparts. Female like male but head is brownish-grey. Large, stout, conical bill. Four subspecies have been described.

DISTRIBUTION: Found on Isabela, Santa Cruz, Santa Fé, Fernandina, Santiago, Floreana, Marchena, Pinta and Rábida. It is not known if it breeds on San Cristóbal, although birds have been seen there. It is extinct on Pinzón. Prefers the highlands, although can occasionally be found feeding in the transitional zone and the coast. In Marchena breeds in the lowlands.

FOOD: Feeds on insects that are found by looking under leaves or excavating branches. Also feeds upon fruits of native plants.

MEDIUM TREE-FINCH *Camarhynchus pauper*   **Plate p. 61**

Sp: Pinzón Mediano de Árbol

STATUS: Endemic

WEIGHT: 16 g.

IDENTIFICATION: Male has black head with dark greyish-brown upperparts and yellow-olive underparts. Female like male but head is greyish-brown. Medium-sized, pale, conical bill.

DISTRIBUTION: Only found on Floreana, higher than 300 m above sea level.

FOOD: Feeds on insects that it finds by looking under twigs and leaves, or digging in the bark of trees. Also feeds on nectar, young buds and leaves and caterpillars.

SMALL TREE-FINCH *Camarhynchus parvulus*   **Plate p. 61**

Sp: Pinzón Pequeño de Árbol

STATUS: Endemic.

WEIGHT: 13 g.

IDENTIFICATION: By far the smallest of the tree-finches. Male has black head, neck, breast and upper back, olivaceous grey-brown upperparts and lighter, yellowish underparts. Some have a few streaks. Female like male but greyer-brown, with head same colour as rest of the body. Bill small, pale and conical. There are two subspecies.

DISTRIBUTION: Found on Isabela, Fernandina, Santa Cruz, Santiago, San Cristóbal, Floreana, Baltra, Santa Fé, Pinzón, and Rábida. Has been seen on Pinta but it is not known if there is a breeding population there. Found mostly in the highlands and the transitional zone.

FOOD: Feeds on insects that it finds by looking under twigs, leaves, and digging in the bark of trees. Also feeds on nectar, young buds and leaves and caterpillars.

Genus *Cactospiza*

Woodpecker and Mangrove Finches show no differences in colour between males and females. The songs of the two species of *Cactospiza* are very different from other finches, but the whistle resembles that of other species.

WOODPECKER FINCH *Cactospiza pallida*   Plate p. 61

Sp: Pinzón Artesano

STATUS: Endemic.

WEIGHT: 20 g.

IDENTIFICATION: No differences between male and female. Upperparts greyish olive. Underparts light olive with no streaks. Shows no black at all in plumage. Long, stout bill, with slightly decurved upper mandible. There are two subspecies.

DISTRIBUTION: Found on Isabela, Santa Cruz, Santiago, Pinzón and San Cristóbal. There could also be a breeding population on Fernandina. Has also been seen on Floreana, Pinta, Baltra and Rábida. Prefers the highlands, although can also be found in the transitional and coastal zones.

FOOD: Displays a uniquely developed ability to use tools to obtain its food. Is regularly seen to use twigs or cactus spines to extract larvae, pupae or termites from holes. Looks under leaves, digs under rocks, and excavates in wood, looking for its favourite food, beetles. In the coast excavates in *Opuntia*. May climb up and down trees in the manner of a nuthatch.

VOICE: The song is a succession of seven to eight or more notes, with a *chur* and a high-pitched *see* added frequently as in other finch species (Lack 1945).

MANGROVE FINCH *Cactospiza heliobates*   Plate p. 61

Sp: Pinzón del Manglar

STATUS: Endemic (rare).

WEIGHT: 18 g.

IDENTIFICATION: Very similar in shape and general appearance to Woodpecker Finch, but shows some streaking on the underparts, is slightly browner in appearance, and has a lighter, smaller bill.

DISTRIBUTION: Very restricted: found only in the mangrove swamps of Isabela. Formerly found on Fernandina, but apparently now extinct there.

FOOD: Feeds in the same way as Woodpecker Finch, mainly on insects. Has been seen to use a tool.

VOICE: This species has a di- or trisyllabic song. Each syllable is repeated three times over in sequence, *tur-tur, tur-tur, tur-tur* or *tur-tur-tur, tur-tur-tur, tur-tur-tur.*

Genus *Certhidia*

WARBLER FINCH *Certhidia olivacea*   **Plate p. 61**

Sp: Pinzón Cantor
STATUS: Endemic.
WEIGHT: 8 g.
IDENTIFICATION: By far the smallest of all the finches, with a sharp, thin bill, more like a warbler than a finch. No difference in colour between the sexes. Has olive-grey upperparts and light olive, buff or sometimes whitish underparts. Males of some populations (mainly on Santiago and Santa Cruz) have traces of orange on the chin and breast. There are eight subspecies.
DISTRIBUTION: Found on all the islands except for Daphne, and may be found in all the zones.
FOOD: Searches leaves, twigs and ground for small insects. Also goes for aerial excursions in search of flying insects. Can occasionally feed on nectar (often on Genovesa) and green leaves.
VOICE: The basic and derive songs of this species are very elaborate. An intricate whistle precedes the basic song.

Family Parulidae

YELLOW WARBLER *Dendroica petechia aureolla*   **Plate p. 56**

Sp: Canario María
STATUS: Resident (endemic subspecies, also on Cocos Islands).
IDENTIFICATION: Length 12 cm. The only member of the New World wood-warblers to live on the islands, and the only bright yellow passerine found there. Male has plain olive-green upperparts, with wings showing darker feather centres; bright golden-yellow face and underparts, with rusty-red streaks along the flanks and sides of chest. Unlike North American races of the species, has a rusty crown. Female similar to northern subspecies, with olive head and upperparts washed with grey, greyish breast, and paler yellowish belly, lacking rusty markings.
DISTRIBUTION: Found on all the islands from the shoreline up to the highest points.
BREEDING: Reproduces during the rainy season (December to May). The nest is cup-shaped and placed in trees. The female incubates.
FOOD: Feeds on insects. It is very common to see several birds feeding on flies on the rocks during low tide.
VOICE: Highly variable, though usually including several high-pitched *swee* notes on the same pitch, followed by a short warbling.

Yellow Warbler at the nest

BLACKPOLL WARBLER *Dendroica striata*   **Plate p. 56**
Sp: Reinita Rayada
STATUS: Vagrant.
IDENTIFICATION: Length 14 cm. Breeding male distinctive, with black cap, white cheeks and strongly streaked sides. Breeding female is duller overall, slightly greenish on upperparts. Autumn adults and immatures (most likely plumage for the Galápagos) have greenish-brown mantle, black wing-coverts and pale greenish-yellow underparts.
DISTRIBUTION: A single record from 1976.

Subfamily Thraupidae

SUMMER TANAGER *Piranga rubra*   **Plate p. 57**
Sp: Cardenal Migratorio
STATUS: Vagrant.
IDENTIFICATION: Length 20 cm. Large, bulky, finch-like bird, with distinctive heavy bill. In summer plumage male and female alike: greyish-olive upperparts, yellow-orange underparts. In winter plumage the male is a uniform red.
DISTRIBUTION: A single, mummified bird was found on Española in 1963. One bird has also been seen on Wolf, and other tanagers, probably this species, have been reported from Santa Cruz.

Subfamily Cardinalinae

ROSE-BREASTED GROSBEAK *Pheucticus ludovicianus* **Plate p. 57**
Sp: Picogordio Degollado
STATUS: Vagrant.
IDENTIFICATION: Length 20 cm. Large, very bulky finch, with huge bill. Female is generally brown, with a streaked breast, and bars on the crown. The wing-linings are orange-yellow. Male has black upperparts and throat, white underparts with a conspicuous red V-shaped patch on breast, red wing-linings and white wing-bars.
DISTRIBUTION: Has been reported from Genovesa and Fernandina.

INDIGO BUNTING *Passerina cyanea* **Plate p. 57**
Sp: Azulillo
STATUS: Vagrant.
IDENTIFICATION: Length 14 cm. Indigo-blue breeding male unmistakable. Female dull brown above, lightly streaked below on buffy underparts. Immature resembles female, while autumn/winter male may have blue tinges to generally brown plumage.
DISTRIBUTION: An uncommon visitor to northern South America from North America, Indigo Bunting has been recorded once in the Galápagos.

Family Icteridae

BOBOLINK *Dolichonyx oryzivorus* **Plate p. 57**
Sp: Tordo Arrocero
STATUS: Migrant (possible resident on San Cristóbal).
IDENTIFICATION: Length 18 cm. In breeding plumage, male is all black below, hindneck buff, fading to white, with white rump and scapulars. Female is buff-brown, heavily streaked on back, sides and rump. Immatures and autumn adult males resemble breeding female, but are darker above and more buffish below. All plumages have sharply pointed tail feathers.
DISTRIBUTION: Has been reported from San Cristóbal, Floreana, Santiago, Santa Cruz, Genovesa and Española. Common from October to December, but has also been found in July and August. Prefers the highlands.

BIBLIOGRAPHY

Abbott, I.J., Abbott, L.K., and Grant, P.R. 1977. Comparative ecology of Galápagos ground finches. *Ecol. Monographs* 47: 151–184.

Alatabo, R. 1982. Bird species distribution in the Galápagos and other archipelagos: competition or chance? *Ecology* 63 (4): 881–887.

Anderson, D.J. 1989. Differential responses of boobies and other seabirds in the Galápagos to the 1986–87 El Niño Southern Oscillation event. *Marine Ecology Progress*, Series 52: 209–216.

Anderson, D. J., and Fortner, S. 1988. Waved albatross egg neglect and associated mosquito ectoparasitism. *Condor* 90: 727–729.

Anderson, D.J. 1991. Apparent predator-limited distribution of Galápagos Red-footed Boobies *Sula sula. Ibis* 133: 26–29.

Arnbom, T.A. 1987. Distribution and behavior of pelagic birds around the Galápagos Islands. *Report to CDRS.* CDRS files, Galápagos.

Ashmole, N.P., and Ashmole, N.J. 1967. Comparative feeding ecology of seabirds of a tropical oceanic island. *Bull. Peabody Mus. Nat. Hist.* 24: 1–131.

Bailey, A. 1961. Dusky and swallow–tailed gulls of the Galápagos Islands. *Museum Pictorial,* No. 15. Denver Museum of Natural History.

Baptista, L, and Trail, P. 1988. On the origin of Darwin finches. *Auk* 105: 663–671.

Barber, R.T., and Chavez, F.P. 1983. Biological consequences of El Niño. *Science* 222: 1203–1210.

Barrass, R. 1978. *Scientists Must Write: a guide to better writing for scientists, engineers and students.* Chapman and Hall. London.

Boag, P.T., and Grant, P.R. 1981. Intense natural selection in a population of Darwin's finches (Geospizinae) in the Galápagos. *Science* 214: 82–85.

Boersma, D. 1978. Breeding patterns of Galápagos penguins as an indicator of oceanographic conditions. *Science* 200: 1489–1493.

Bowman, R. I. 1983. The evolution of song in Darwin's Finches, in R. I. Bowman, M. Berson and A.E. Leviton (eds.), *Patterns of evolution in Galápagos organisms.* American Association for the Advancement of Science, Pacific Division. San Francisco, California.

Carne, M.A. 1983. Oceanographic events during El Niño. *Science* 222: 1189–1195.

Castro, I.C. 1988–1989. Reports to the CDRS on the dark-rumped petrel projects in Santa Cruz and Floreana. CDRS files. Galápagos.

Castro, I.C. 1989. Censo de pinguinos y cormoranes. Report to the CDRS. CDRS files. Galápagos.

Castro, I.C. 1989. Proteccion de Golondrinas de tormenta en el islote Pitt, Isla San Cristóbal. Report to the CDRS. CDRS files. Galápagos.

Castro, I.C. 1988 and 1989. Reporte del censo de flamencos. Report to the CDRS. CDRS files. Galápagos.

Castro, I.C. 1988 and 1989. Garrapateros. Internal Report to the CDRS. CDRS files. Galápagos.

Christian, K.A. 1980. Cleaning/feeding symbiosis between birds and reptiles of the Galápagos Islands: new observations of inter–island variability. *Auk* 97 (4): 887–889.

Cox A. 1983. Ages of the Galápagos Islands, in R. I. Bowman, M. Berson and A.E. Leviton (eds.), *Patterns of evolution in Galápagos organisms.* American Association for the Advancement of Science, Pacific Division. San Francisco, California.

Cruz, F., and Cruz, J. 1985. The effect of El Niño on the breeding of the dark–rumped petrel on Cerro Pajas, Floreana, in G. Robinson and M.E. del Pino, *El Niño en las islas Galápagos.* Quito, Ecuador.

Cruz, J.B., and Cruz, F. 1987. Conservation of the dark–rumped petrel *Pterodroma phaeopygia* in the Galápagos Islands, Ecuador. *Biol. Cons.* 42 (4): 303–311.

Cruz, J.B. 1982–1987. Semestral and annual Reports to the CDRS on the dark–rumped petrel. CDRS files. Galápagos.

Curry, R.L. 1985. Breeding and survival of Galápagos mockingbirds during El Niño, in G. Robinson and M.E. del Pino, *El Niño en las islas Galápagos.* Quito, Ecuador.

Curry, R.L., and Stoleson, S.H. 1988. New bird records from the Galápagos associated with the El Niño-Southern Oscillation. *Condor* 90: 505–507.

De Groot, R.S. 1983. Origin, status and ecology of the owls in Galápagos. *Ardea* 71 (2): 167–182.

De Vries, T. 1975. The breeding biology of the Galápagos hawk (*Buteo galapagoensis*). *Le Gerfaut* 65: 29–57.

Eliasson, U. 1984. Native Climax forests, in Perry (ed.), *Key Environments: Galápagos*. Pergamon Press.

Faaborg, J., De Vries, T., Paterson, A.B., and Griffin, C.R. 1980. Preliminary observations on the occurrence and evolution of polyandry in the Galápagos Hawk (*Buteo galapagoensis*). *Auk* 97: 581–590.
Franklin, A.B., Clark, D.A., and Clark, D.B. 1979. Ecology and behavior of the Galápagos rail. *Wilson Bull.* 91 (2): 202–221.

Gibbs, H.L., Grant P.R., and Weiland, J. 1984. Breeding of Darwin's finches at an unusually early age in an El Niño year. *Auk* 104: 872–874.
Gibbs, H.L., Latta, S., and Gibbs, J. 1987. Effects of the 82–83 El Niño event on blue–footed and masked booby populations on Isla Daphne Major, Galápagos. *Condor* 89: 440–442.
Gibbs, H.L., and Gibbs, J. 1987. Prey robbery by non–breeding magnificent frigate birds (*Fregata magnificens*). *Wilson Bull.* 999 (1): 101–104.
Gibbs, H.L., and Grant, P.R. 1987. Oscillating selection and Darwin's finches. *Nature* 327 (6122): 511–513.
Gifford, E.W. 1919. Field notes on the land birds of the Galápagos and of Cocos Island, Costa Rica. *Proc. Calif. Acad. Sci.* Ser. 4, No. 2: 189–258.
Grant, P.R. 1984. Recent research on the evolution of land birds on the Galápagos. *Biol. J. Linn. Soc.* 21: 113–136.
Grant, P.R., and Grant, K.T. 1979. Breeding and feeding ecology of the Galápagos dove. *Condor* 81: 397–403.
Grant, P.R., and Grant, N. 1979. Breeding and feeding of Galápagos mockingbirds *Nesomimus parvulus. Auk* 96: 723–736.
Grant, P.R., Smith, J.N.M., Grant, B.R., Abbott, I.J., and Abbott, L.K. 1975. Finch numbers, owl predation and plant dispersal on Isla Daphne Major, Galápagos. *Oecologia* 19: 239–257.
Grant, P.R., and Grant, B.R. 1985. Responses of Darwin's Finches to unusual rainfall, in G. Robinson and M.E. del Pino, *El Niño en las islas Galápagos*. Quito, Ecuador.
Grant, P.R. 1986. *Ecology and Evolution of Darwin's Finches*. Princeton University Press.
Grant, B.R., and Grant, P.R. 1989. *Evolutionary Dynamics of a Natural Population. The Large Cactus Finch of the Galapagos*. University of Chicago Press.

Hailman, J.P. 1963. Why is the lava gull the color of lava? *Condor* 65: 528.
Hailman, J.P. 1964. The Galápagos swallow–tailed gull is nocturnal. *Wilson Bull.* 76: 347–354.
Hailman, J.P. 1965. Cliff nesting adaptations of the Galápagos swallow–tailed gull. *Wilson Bull.* 77: 346–362.
Hailman, J.P. 1966. Strange gull of the Galápagos. *Audubon Magazine*. 68: 180–184.
Hailman, J.P. 1968. Behavioural studies of the swallow–tailed gull. *Noticias de Galápagos*. 11: 9–12.
Hamman, O. 1981. Plant community of the Galápagos Islands. *Dansk Botanisk Archiv* 34: 1–63.
Hamman, O. 1984. Changes and threats to the vegetation, in Perry (ed.), *Key Environments: Galápagos*. Pergamon Press.
Harris, M.P. 1968. Egg eating by Galápagos mockingbirds. *Condor* 70: 269–270.
Harris, M.P. 1969. The biology of storm petrels in the Galápagos Islands. *Proc. Calif. Acad. Sci.*, Ser. 4, No. 37 (4): 95–166.
Harris, M.P. 1969. Factors influencing the breeding cycle of the red–billed tropicbird in the Galápagos Islands. *Ardea* 57: 149–
Harris, M.P. 1969. Breeding seasons of seabirds in the Galápagos Islands. *J. Zool. London.* 159: 145–165.
Harris, M.P. 1969. Food as factor controlling the breeding of *Puffinus l'herminieri. Ibis* 111: 139–156.
Harris, M.P. 1970. Breeding ecology of the swallow–tailed gull. *Auk* 87: 215–243.
Harris, M.P. 1973. The Galápagos avifauna. *Condor* 75: 265–278.
Harris, M.P. 1973. The biology of the waved albatross *Diomedea irorata* of the Hood Island, Galápagos. *Ibis* 115: 483–510.
Harris, M.P. 1974. *A Field Guide to the Birds of Galapagos*. Collins. London.
Harrison, P. 1983. *Seabirds: an identification guide*. Croom Helm Ltd. Beckenham.
Hayman, P., Marchant, J., and Prater, T. 1986. *Shorebirds: an identification guide to the waders of the world*. Christopher Helm Ltd. London.

Hernandez, C., and De Vries, T. 1985. Fluctuaciones en la poblacion de fragatas, *Fregata minor*, en Bahia Darwin, Genovesa durante 1975–1983, in G. Robinson and M.E. del Pino, *El Niño en las islas Galápagos*. Quito, Ecuador.

Jackson, M.H. 1985. *Galápagos: a natural history guide*. The University of Calgary Press. Calgary, Canada.

King, W. 1981. *Red Data Book*. ICBP–IUCN. Cambridge.
Koster, F., and Koster, H. 1985. Twelve days among the vampire finches of Wolf Island, in in G. Robinson and M.E. del Pino, *El Niño en las islas Galápagos*. Quito, Ecuador.
Kushlan, J.A. 1983. Pair formation behaviour of the Galápagos lava heron, *Butorides striatus/sundevalli*. *Wilson Bull*. 95 (1): 118–121.

Lack, D. 1945. The Galápagos finches: a study in variation. *Calif. Acad. Sci. Occas. Papers*, No. 21.
Lack, D. 1950. Breeding seasons in the Galápagos. *Ibis* 92: 268.
Leveque, R., Bowman, R., and Billeb, S. 1966. Migrants in the Galápagos area. *Condor* 68: 81–101.

Madge, S., and Burn, H. 1988. *Wildfowl: an identification guide to the ducks, geese and swans of the world*. Christopher Helm Ltd. London.
Merlen, G. 1988. Sea Birds of Galápagos and Land birds of the Galápagos archipelago. Manuscripts used for the guides course. GNPS, Galápagos.
Moll, E.J. 1990. A report on the distribution of introduced plants on Santa Cruz Island, Galápagos. Botany Department Publication. University of Cape Town, R.S.A.
Morris, P. 1979. Rats in the diet of the barn owl (*Tyto alba*). *J. Zool*. 189: 540–545.

Naranjo, P. 1985. El fenomeno de El Niño y sus efectos en el clima del Ecuador, in G. Robinson and M.E. del Pino, *El Niño en las islas Galápagos*. Quito, Ecuador.
Nelson, J.B. 1969. Breeding ecology of the red-footed boobies in the Galápagos. *J. Ann. Zool*. 38: 101–190.
Nisbet, I.C.T. 1960. Notes on the American purple gallinule. *British Birds* 53: 146–149.
Nisbet, I.C.T. 1960. Notes on the rose-breasted grosbeak. *British Birds* 53: 149–152.

Palacios, J. 1989. Informe sobre alimentacion del Garrapatero en la zona agricola de la Isla Santa Cruz. Report to the CDRS. CDRS files. Galápagos.
Peterson, R.T. 1967. The Galápagos. *National Geographic Magazine* 131: 541–585.
Porter, D.M. 1976. Geography and dispersal of Galápagos Islands vascular plants. Nature 264: 745–746.

Rechten, C. 1985. The waved albatros in 1983 – El Niño leads to complete breeding failure, in G. Robinson and M.E. del Pino, *El Niño en las islas Galápagos*. Quito, Ecuador.
Reeder, W.G., and Reichert, S.E. 1975. Vegetation change along an altitudinal gradient. Santa Cruz Island, Galápagos. *Biotropica* 7:162–175.
Reville, B. 1988. Effects of spacing and synchrony on breeding success in the great frigatebird (*Fregata minor*). *Auk* 105: 252–259.
Robalino, M. 1985. Registros meteorologicos de la Estacion Cientifica Charles Darwin para 1982–1983, in G. Robinson and M.E. del Pino, *El Niño en las islas Galápagos*. Quito, Ecuador.
Robbins, C.S., Bruun, B., and Zim, H.S. 1983. *Birds of North America: a guide to field identification*. Golden Press. New York.
Robert, M., McNail, R., and Leduc, A. Conditions and significance of night feeding in shorebirds and other waterbirds in a tropical lagoon. *Auk* 106: 94–101.
Robinson, G.R. 1987. Negative effects of the 82–83 El Niño event on Galápagos marine life. *Oceanus* 30 (2): 42–48.
Rosemberg, D.K. 1987. 1989. Impact of introduced hervivores on the Galápagos rail (*Laterallus spilonotus*). Report to the CDRS. CDRS files, Galápagos.
Rosemberg D.K., and Harcourt, S. 1987. Population sizes and potential conservation problems of the endemic Galápagos penguin and flightless cormorant. *Noticias de Galápagos*, No. 45: 32–34.

Schluter, D. 1982. Distribution of Galápagos ground finches along an altitudinal gradient: the importance of food supply. *Ecology* 63 (5): 1504–1517.

Simkim, T. 1984. Geology of the Galápagos Islands, in Perry (ed.), *Key Environments: Galápagos*. Pergamon Press.

Smith, J., Grant, P.R., Grant, B.R., Abbott I.J., and Abbott, L.K. 1978. Seasonal variation in feeding habits of Darwin's ground finches. *Ecology* 59 (6): 1137–1150.

Snow, B.K. 1966. Observations on the behaviour and ecology of the flightless cormorant. *Ibis* 108 (2): 265–280.

Snow, B.K., and Snow, D.W. 1968. Behaviour of the swallow–tailed gull of the Galápagos. *Condor* 70: 252–264.

Snow, B.K., and Snow, D.W. 1969. Observations on the lava gull. *Ibis* 111: 30–

Snow, D.W. 1965. The breeding of Audubon's shearwater in the Galápagos. *Auk* 82: 591–597.

Snow, D.W. 1965. The breeding of the red–billed tropicbird in the Galápagos Islands. *Condor* 67: 210–214.

Snow, D.W., and Snow, B.K. 1967. The breeding cycle of the swallow–tailed gull *Creagrus furcatus*. *Ibis* 109: 14–24.

Snow, D.W., and Nelson, J.B. 1984. Evolution and adaptations of Galápagos seabirds. *Biol. J. Linn. Soc.* 21: 137–155.

Soothill, E., and Soothill, R. 1982. *Wading Birds of the World*. Blandford. Poole, Dorset.

Sosa, A.C. 1985. Fluctuaciones en las poblaciones de aves en Quinta Playa, Isla Isabela, Galápagos, in G. Robinson and M.E. del Pino, *El Niño en las islas Galápagos*. Quito, Ecuador.

Steadman, D., and Zousmer, S. 1988. *Galápagos: discovery on Darwin's islands*. Smithsonian Institution Press. Washington, D.C.

Tindle, R.W. 1984. Evolution of breeding strategies in the flightless cormorant (*Nanopterum harrisi*) of the Galápagos. *Biol. J. Linn. Soc.* 21: 157–164.

Tindle, R.W., and Tindle, L.E. 1978. Studies of the greater flamingo, *Phoenicopterus ruber ruber*, in the Galápagos Islands. Charles Darwin Research Station Annual Report.

Townsend, H. 1929. The flightless cormorant in captivity. *Auk* 46: 211–213.

Trillmich, F., Trillmich, K., Arnold, A., and Limberger, D. 1983. The breeding season of the flightless cormorant, at Cabo Hammond, Fernandina, Galápagos. *Ibis* 125(2): 221–223.

Tupiza, A. 1985. Cambios en la laguna de El Cementerio y en Puerto Villamil, Isla Isabela, causados por el fenómeno de El Niño en 1982–83, in G. Robinson and M.E. del Pino, *El Niño en las islas Galápagos*. Quito, Ecuador.

Vagvolgyi, J., and Vagvolgyi, M. 1989. The taxonomic status of the small ground finch *Geospiza* (aves Emberizidae) of Genovesa Island, Galápagos and its relevance to interespecific competition. *Auk* 106: 144–148.

Valle, C. 1983. Census of cormorants and penguins around Fernandina and Isabela. *CDRS Informe Anual*. 1986: 32–34.

Valle, C. 1985. Alteracion de las poblaciones del cormoran no volador, el pinguino y otras aves marinas en Galápagos por efecto de El Niño 1982–83 y su subsecuente recuperacion, in G. Robinson and M.E. del Pino, *El Niño en las islas Galápagos*. Quito, Ecuador.

Valle, C. 1988. Estado actual de las poblaciones de aves marinas en Islote Pitt, Galápagos, Ecuador. Report to the CDRS. CDRS files, Galápagos.

Valle, C., and Coulter, M. 1987. Present status of the flightless cormorant, Galápagos penguin and greater flamingo populations in the Galápagos Islands, Ecuador after the 82–83 El Niño. *Condor* 89 (2): 276–287.

Valle, C., Cruz, F., Cruz, J.B., Merlen, G., and Coulter, M.C. 1987. The impact of the 1982–1983 El Niño–Southern Oscillation on seabirds on the Galápagos islands, Ecuador. *J. Geoph. Res.* 92 (C13): 14437–14444.

Voous, K.H., and De Vries, T. 1978. Systematic place and geographic history of the Galápagos hawk (*Buteo galapagoensis*). *Le Gerfaut* 68: 245–252.

Wyrtki, K. 1975. El Niño: The dynamic response of the Equatorial Pacific Ocean to atmospheric forcing. *J. Phys. Oceanogr.* 5 (4): 572.

Wyrtki, K. 1977. Sea level during the 1972 El Niño. *J. Phys. Oceanogr.* 7 (6): 779.

CHECKLIST OF GALÁPAGOS BIRDS

Observer(s) name(s):

	Island	Habitat	Date	Time	Observations
Pied-billed Grebe *Podilymbus podiceps*					
Galápagos Penguin *Spheniscus mendiculus*					
Wandering Albatross *Diomedea exulans*					
Waved Albatross *Diomedea irrorata*					
Black-footed Albatross *Diomedea nigripes*					
Black-browed Albatross *Diomedea melanophris*					
Southern Giant Petrel *Macronetes giganteus*					
Southern Fulmar *Fulmarus glacialodes*					
Cape Petrel *Daption capense*					
White-winged Petrel *Pterodroma leucoptera*					
Dark-rumped Petrel *Pterodroma leucoptera*					
Dove Prion *Pachyptila desolata*					
Parkinson's Black Petrel *Procellaria parkinsoni*					
Wedge-tailed Shearwater *Puffinus pacificus*					
Flesh-footed Shearwater *Puffinus carneipes*					
Sooty Shearwater *Puffinus griseus*					
Audubon's Shearwater *Puffinus lherminieri subularis*					
Elliot's Storm-petrel *Oceanites gracilis galapagoensis*					
White-faced Storm-petrel *Pelagodroma marina*					
White-bellied Storm-petrel *Fregatta grallaria*					
Wedge-rumped Storm-petrel *Oceanodroma tethys tethys*					
Madeiran Storm-petrel *Oceanodroma castro*					
Leach's Storm-petrel *Oceanodroma leucorhoa*					
Markham's Storm-petrel *Oceanodroma markhami*					
Black Storm-petrel *Oceanodroma melania*					
Red-billed Tropicbird *Phaethon aethereus*					
Magnificent Frigatebird *Fregata magnificens magnificens*					
Great Frigatebird *Fregata minor ridgwayi*					
Blue-footed Booby *Sula nebouxii excisa*					
Masked Booby *Sula dactyla granti*					
Red-footed Booby *Sula sula websteri*					
Flightless Cormorant *Nannopterum harrisi*					
Brown Pelican *Pelecanus occidentalis urinator*					
Black-bellied Whistling-duck *Dendrocygna autumnalis*					
White-cheeked Pintail *Anas bahamensis galapagensis*					
Blue-winged Teal *Anas discors*					
Greater Flamingo *Phoenicopterus ruber*					

	Island	Habitat	Date	Time	Observations
Snowy Egret *Leucophoyx thula*					
Great Blue Heron *Ardea herodias*					
Great Egret *Casmerodius albus*					
Cattle Egret *Bulbulcus ibis*					
Striated Heron *Butorides striatus*					
Lava Heron *Butorides sundevalli*					
Yellow-crowned Night Heron *Nyctanassa violacea pauper*					
Black-crowned Night Heron *Nycticorax nycticorax*					
Osprey *Pandion haliaetus*					
Galápagos Hawk *Buteo galapagoensis*					
Peregrine Falcon *Falco peregrinus*					
Galápagos Crake *Laterallus spilonotus*					
Sora Rail *Porzana carolina*					
Paint-billed Crake *Neocrex erythrops*					
Purple Gallinule *Porphyrula martinica*					
Common Gallinule *Gallinula chloropus*					
Marbled Godwit *Limosa fedoa*					
Whimbrel *Numenius phaeopus hudsonicus*					
Greater Yellowlegs *Tringa melanoleuca*					
Lesser Yellowlegs *Tringa flavipes*					
Solitary Sandpiper *Tringa solitaria*					
Spotted Sandpiper *Actitis macularia*					
Wandering Tattler *Heteroscelus incanum*					
Willet *Catoptropherus semipalmatus*					
Ruddy Turnstone *Arenaria interpres*					
Black Turnstone *Arenaria melanocephala*					
Short-billed Dowitcher *Limnodromus griseus*					
Surfbird *Aphriza virgata*					
Red Knot *Calidris canutus*					
Sanderling *Calidris alba*					
Semipalmated Sandpiper *Calidris pusilla*					
Western Sandpiper *Calidris mauri*					
Least Sandpiper *Calidris minutilla*					
White-rumped Sandpiper *Calidris fuscicollis*					
Baird's Sandpiper *Calidris bairdii*					
Pectoral Sandpiper *Calidris melanotos*					
Stilt Sandpiper *Micropalama himantopus*					
Wilson's Phalarope *Phalaropus tricolor*					
Red-necked Phalarope *Phalaropus lobatus*					
Red Phalarope *Phalaropus fulicarius*					
American Oystercatcher *Haematopus palliatus galapagensis*					
Black-necked Stilt *Himantopus (himantopus) mexicanus*					

	Island	Habitat	Date	Time	Observations
American Golden Plover *Pluvialis dominica*					
Black-bellied Plover *Pluvialis squatarola*					
Semipalmated Plover *Charadrius semipalmatus*					
Wilson's Plover *Charadrius wilsonia*					
Killdeer *Chardrius vociferus*					
Southern Black-backed Gull *Larus dominicanus*					
Lava Gull *Larus fuliginosus*					
Laughing Gull *Larus atricilla*					
Franklin's Gull *Larus pipixcan*					
Swallow-tailed Gull *Larus furcatus*					
Black Tern *Chlidonias niger*					
Royal Tern *Sterna maxima*					
Common Tern *Sterna hirundo*					
Sooty Tern *Sterna fuscata*					
White Tern *Gygis alba*					
Common Noddy *Anous stolidus galapagensis*					
South Polar Skua *Catharacta maccormicki*					
Pomarine Skua *Stercorarius pomarinus*					
Eared Dove *Zenaida auriculata*					
Galápagos Dove *Zenaida galapagoensis*					
Black-billed Cuckoo *Coccyzus erythropthalmus*					
Dark-billed Cuckoo *Coccyzus melacoryphus*					
Smooth-billed Ani *Crotophaga ani*					
Barn Owl *Tyto alba punctatissima*					
Short-eared Owl *Asio flammeus galapagoensis*					
Common Nighthawk *Chordeiles minor*					
Chimney Swift *Chaetura pelagica*					
Belted Kingfisher *Ceryle alcyon*					
Vermillion Flycatcher *Pyrocephalus rubinus*					
Galápagos Flycatcher *Myiarchus magnirostris*					
Eastern Kingbird *Tyrannus tyrannus*					
Red-eyed Vireo *Vireo olivaceus*					
Galápagos Mockingbird *Nesomimus parvulus*					
Charles Mockingbird *Nesomimus trifasciatus*					
Hood Mockingbird *Nesomimus macdonaldi*					
Chatham Mockingbird *Nesomimus melanotis*					
Cedar Waxwing *Bombycilla cedrorum*					
Purple Martin *Progne subis*					
Galápagos Martin *Progne modesta modesta*					
Sand Martin *Riparia riparia*					
Barn Swallow *Hirundo rustica*					
Cliff Swallow *Petrochelidon pyrrhonota*					

	Island	Habitat	Date	Time	Observations
Large Ground-finch *Geospiza magnirostris*					
Medium Ground-finch *Geospiza fortis*					
Small Ground-finch *Geospiza fuliginosa*					
Sharp-beaked Ground-finch *Geospiza difficilis*					
Common Cactus-finch *Geospiza scandens*					
Large Cactus-finch *Geospiza conirostris*					
Vegetarian Finch *Platyspiza crassirostris*					
Large Tree-finch *Camarhynchus psittacula*					
Medium Tree-finch *Camarhynchus pauper*					
Small Tree-finch *Camarhynchus parvulus*					
Woodpecker Finch *Cactospiza pallida*					
Mangrove Finch *Cactospiza heliobates*					
Warbler Finch *Certhidia olivacea*					
Yellow Warbler *Dendroica petechia aureolla*					
Blackpoll Warbler *Dendroica striata*					
Summer Tanager *Piranga rubra*					
Rose-breasted Grosbeak *Pheucticus ludovicianus*					
Indigo Bunting *Passerina cyanea*					
Bobolink *Dolichonyx oryzivorus*					

In case of new sightings or sightings of rare birds, please send records to Isabel Castro, Department of Ecology, Massey University, New Zealand. Thank you.

INDEX

Numbers in bold refer to plate pages.

143